Other Books by
S. MICHAEL WILCOX

*What the Scriptures Teach
Us about Raising a Child*

*What the Scriptures Teach
Us about Prosperity*

What the
SCRIPTURES
Teach Us about
ADVERSITY

S. MICHAEL WILCOX

DESERET
BOOK
SALT LAKE CITY, UTAH

Library of Congress Cataloging-in-Publication Data

Wilcox, S. Michael.
    What the scriptures teach us about adversity / S. Michael Wilcox.
       p. cm.
    Includes bibliographical references and index.
    ISBN 978-1-60641-811-6 (hardbound : alk. paper)   1. Suffering—Biblical teaching.
2. Suffering—Religious aspects—The Church of Jesus Christ of Latter-day Saints.
3. The Church of Jesus Christ of Latter-day Saints—Doctrines. I. Title.
    BX8643.S93W55 2010
    248.8'6—dc22   2010017610

Printed in the United States of America
Worzalla Publishing Co., Stevens Point, WI

10 9 8 7 6 5 4 3 2 1

—~~~—

May God grant unto you that your burdens may be
light, through the joy of his Son.
Alma 33:23

CONTENTS

Introduction: The Commonality of Adversity 1

1. Thou Knowest the Greatness of God 6

2. It Is Finished 23

3. Under the Juniper Tree 37

4. Thy Friends Do Stand by Thee 45

5. Thou Art Not Yet as Job 53

6. Tears upon the Mountains 72

7. In the Days When the Judges Ruled 86

8. Such As I Have 96

9. Sufficient unto the Day 103

10. How Many Loaves Have Ye? 119

CONTENTS

11. When Paradise Is Lost 126

12. The Sword or the Angel 137

13. That Our Burdens May Be Light 144

    Notes 147

    Index 149

—∿—

As for the perils which I am called to pass through, they
seem but a small thing to me. . . . Deep water is what I
am wont to swim in. It all has become a second nature to
me; . . . for . . . the God of my fathers delivered me out of
them all, and will deliver me from henceforth.

Joseph Smith, in Doctrine & Covenants 127:2

THE COMMONALITY OF ADVERSITY

When I was growing up I often heard my grandfather say there were only two things in life nobody escaped—death and taxes. My grandfather would say this with an ironic half-smile. Now that I am approaching the age he was when I first heard him utter this piece of folk wisdom, I find that I agree with him. And I would add another inevitability to the list—that of adversity. Each of us faces trials, setbacks, disappointments, doubts, discouragements, and spiritual droughts. These may range from the occasional unaccountable depressions we feel to the tragic, life-shattering, dream-ending episodes that make real our worst fears.

I did not know when I first wrote this introduction that within a few short months my wife, Laurie, and I would face such a trial. Consistent, perhaps, with the turnings of human destiny, on the day I received the pages of this book for final review, we met with a neurological oncologist, who delivered the news that my beloved Laurie had a stage III inoperable malignant tumor in her brain.

We had discovered there were problems after she experienced a series of seizures. When I saw her in the hospital, the only sign that she recognized me was a smile. I thought at the time, *I will never have a conversation with my wife again.* All efforts to communicate with her ended in futile despair. Over time the swelling from the seizures subsided, and with the reduction in pressure, her normal brain functions returned, but our future is certainly not what we envisioned when I retired to spend more time with her only four months before.

So we begin our journey into the uncertain and often fearful world of adversity. In a brief moment life forever changed. When I first wrote this book, adversity was primarily theology. Now the principles of the scriptures in which I so ardently believe will be challenged by the uncompromising face of reality. I have reread these pages with such thoughts in mind, and though our time in adversity's shadow has just begun, I find a deep sense of comfort and relief arising from the scriptural truths discovered as I wrote the following pages. They are proving equal to the crisis of our lives. I pray they will prove equal to yours.

We are told in sacred places that part of the purpose of our mortal existence is to face such trials to our faith, to our loves, to the very possibility of happiness. As difficult as that may be, our trials are part of the refining. That may, at times, challenge our belief in God—at least in a caring, loving, personal God—as well as our belief in the goodness of others and of mankind in general.

I first tasted grief as a little boy when I witnessed a beloved dog dying behind the generator in the garage at my uncle's ranch, where I stayed during the summer. I learned about cruelty from the bully who terrorized the very air I breathed and caused me to go to school each day gripped in fear. These initial encounters were mild adversities in the vast history of human suffering, but they were mine, and they were the beginning of my acquaintance with the common lot of mankind. My refinement now continues with that single, shattering word: *cancer*.

Our universal history, both as a species and as individuals, is punctuated by the mystery of human suffering. Because we all must pass through these experiences, we would be surprised if the scriptures did not give us counsel, comfort, and preparation for the unavoidable moments we know must come but which nonetheless often take us with amazing poignancy. Searching for that scriptural wisdom is sure to arm us with enduring power and an ability to learn the lessons that life teaches. Though the scriptures cannot remove the pain we may carry with us for a lifetime, they can help us make sense of that pain, at least as much as a mortal can understand the often incomprehensible. They can provide a healing hope to which we must ever cling. Because we are all initiates in the fellowship of pain, the scriptures become our common bond.

Even a cursory examination of sacred writ reveals human anguish, often on a tremendous scale. Ponder, for example, the cries from the souls of some of God's noblest sons and daughters, whose lives were often exemplary and whose love of God is undoubted. Rachel's grief for her barrenness as she watched her sister bear successive sons to Jacob: "Give me children, or else I die" (Genesis 30:1). The pain of her sister, Leah, in an unfulfilled, alienated marriage: "Surely the Lord hath looked upon my affliction; now therefore my husband will love me" (Genesis 29:32). Esau's dawning realization of lost opportunities: "Hast thou not reserved a blessing for me? . . . Hast thou but one blessing, my father? bless me, even me also, O my father" (Genesis 27:36, 38). David's cry upon hearing of his rebellious son's death in the battle for his own crown: "O my son Absalom, my son, my son Absalom! would

God I had died for thee, O Absalom, my son, my son!" (2 Samuel 18:33). Elijah pleading for death in the depths of his own discouragement: "It is enough; now, O Lord, take away my life; for I am not better than my fathers" (1 Kings 19:4). Job sitting upon the ash heap outside his city wishing he had never been born: "Let the day perish wherein I was born. . . . Let that day be darkness. . . . For the thing which I greatly feared is come upon me" (Job 3:3–4, 25). Mary and Martha kneeling before the Savior at the death of Lazarus: "Lord, if thou hadst been here, my brother had not died" (John 11:32). Nephi, deeply aware of his own imperfections, adding to the scriptural record: "O wretched man that I am!" (2 Nephi 4:17). Joseph Smith in Liberty Jail, fighting the feeling of abandonment from the Lord he loved, praying: "O God, where art thou?" (D&C 121:1). And those simple but heart-rending words uttered from the cross by Jesus in the last moments of his life: "My God, my God," and "I thirst" (Mark 15:34; John 19:28).

Where we have no words to express the nature or the depth of adversity, images are left to us, images that need no words. We see Adam and Eve mourning over Cain's treachery and over Abel, the victim of his malice; Joseph led by the Ishmaelites into Egyptian slavery as his brothers unfeelingly ignore his pleas; Jeremiah lowered into the darkness and mire of a dungeon in Jerusalem. We see Rizpah waving the carrion birds away from the bodies of her executed sons. We reflect on the twelve years of anguish endured by the woman with the issue of blood, the thirty-eight years of the man at the pool of Bethesda, the more than forty years endured by the man lame from birth begging at the gate Beautiful. We see the physical pain and the spiritual anguish of the lepers and the sinners who came to Jesus for relief. In some way, great or small, almost every story in the scriptures is a record of struggle, conflict, and opposition, for those are what mortality brings. But there is also triumph, forgiveness, compassion, patience, and endurance—man at his noblest in the face of life's bewildering inconsistencies and injustice. How do we make sense of it all and still sing with the pure faith of a Primary child: "I know my Father lives and loves me too"?[1]

Within the Circumference of an Imperfect World

The totality of human pain cannot fit within the bounds of the human heart; it could find place only in the heart of the Atoning Son, and it caused even him to tremble and shrink, but its many dimensions are measured in the scriptures. When we speak of human suffering, we must realize that only Christ has experienced that totality; we have experienced merely our own petitions of "Abba, Father, all things are possible unto thee; take away this cup from me" (Mark 14:36).

Nevertheless, our adversities are our own, and we must see them through. When they are not our own, only the callous and inhuman fail to respond with sympathetic understanding to the fears and grief of others. No matter what we have faced, are facing now, or may yet face, there will be direction, hope, and comfort in considering the lives and adversities of those who have gone before. If nothing else, we will understand that the finest and most righteous people who have ever lived faced the most crippling, demoralizing, and desperate adversities—as well as little daily frustrations and disappointments. They, too, had to come to grips with the limitations of their own mortality within the circumference of an imperfect world. There is no question that God loved them and that they mattered to him. Likewise, we need not suppose we are less in the eyes of God, either as the recipients of his love or in our individual worthiness. Life brings adversity, and in its own ironic manner of instilling truth, adversity is life's great tutor. Let us turn to those whose wisdom, born of experience, can help us endure, be joyful, hold faith in our hearts, and find healing.

—⟋⟍—

CHAPTER ONE

Hear me, O Lord; for thy lovingkindness
is good: turn unto me according to the multitude
of thy tender mercies.

Psalm 69:16

THOU KNOWEST THE GREATNESS OF GOD

Truths That Need Knowing

When searching the scriptures, we soon notice that certain truths are particularly necessary for us to know in order to receive the full measure of all that life can offer us. There are lessons to be learned, comforts to be granted, and encouragement bestowed. When the Lord has a principle or life lesson he knows we must be aware of, he repeats it time and time again throughout the scriptures. The setting and the characters change, but the essential knowledge remains consistent. It is as if the Lord is saying, "This truth is vital for you. I have placed it in numerous places in the holy record. If you miss it in the Old Testament, perhaps you will notice it in the New. If it has not come to your attention in the Bible, you will find it discussed and illustrated several times in the Book of Mormon. I have placed it also in the Doctrine and Covenants and in the Pearl of Great Price."

Once we have discovered a truth vital to our spiritual survival, its importance is emphasized by its repetition throughout the scriptural text. When we see it illustrated for the first time, it may not penetrate as deeply into our mind and heart as our Father in Heaven might desire, but becoming aware of its existence, we begin to notice it surfacing again and again. This repeated emphasis lets us know how important the truth is and how much we can rely on its promises. Therefore the Lord wants us not only to find the principle but also to realize how it is emphasized. Such is the case with the first great truth regarding adversity we will explore. That truth is the assurance that God can turn any negative of life into a positive. If life takes us into the minus of negative experiences, heaven sends down a vertical line to intersect it and make all things positive. Let us look at a few examples from various places throughout the standard works.

It bears mentioning at the outset that this truth—that God can make all things good—was taught specifically by those who suffered greatly. It is one thing to talk, as a theological exercise, about trials, pain, and adversity, but unless the person doing the teaching has himself or herself been through the fire, there is always a certain element of distance in such discussions. I think it evidence of God's wisdom that the greatest and most often repeated lessons come from those who have experienced the deepest opposition to their happiness and well-being.

"All Things Work Together for Good"

One such was the Apostle Paul. Next to the Savior himself, I can think of no other individual in the New Testament who faced greater adversity and trial than Paul, either inwardly, as a result of his early persecution of the Saints and the distress this caused him later, or outwardly, as he faced persecution and hardship in his years as a missionary for Christ. In his Epistle to the Romans, Paul affirmed, "And we know that all things work together for good to them that love God" (Romans 8:28).

Given time, the Lord can extract the most good out of the most unfortunate of circumstances. Our love of God is more than matched by his love for us. That is why he will not allow negatives to remain negative. He will find a way to change the dynamics of our trials and turn them to blessings. Paul asserted this love of God for us: "Who shall separate us from the love of Christ?" he asked. "Shall tribulation, or distress, or persecution, or famine, or nakedness, or peril, or sword?" (Romans 8:35). All of these Paul knew from experience. Yet he continued with his testimony of God's goodness: "Nay, in all these things we are more than conquerors through him that loved us. For I am persuaded, that neither death, nor life, nor angels, nor principalities, nor powers, nor things present, nor things to come, nor height, nor depth, nor any other creature, shall be able to separate us from the love of God, which is in Christ Jesus our Lord" (Romans 8:37–39).

Paul knew, however, that for the Lord to work his transforming miracles requires patience on our part. Exhibiting patience while in the midst of pain is not easily done, but its fruits are tailored to the difficulty. In this same Epistle to the Romans, Paul masterfully illustrates the manner in which God moves our negatives to the positive side of the equation. Notice how each element in Paul's formula builds on the other. "We glory in tribulations also: knowing that tribulation worketh patience" (Romans 5:3). *Glory* is a strange verb to use in connection with tribulation, but Paul knew by experience that the result would be good, as God promises. God teaches us the good we can expect if we are patient. Notice also that Paul uses in this verse the same verb—*worketh*—that he did in Romans 8 when he promised that all things would *work* for our good. Part of the good work tribulation can accomplish is the patience it can produce.

Paul continues with his formula: "And patience, experience" (Romans 5:4). Though the verb is not stated here, it is implied. Patience will work, or create, *experience*. We must now discern what Paul means by this rich word, especially in light of the fact that the Lord himself would use this very word in responding to the Prophet Joseph Smith while he was incarcerated in Liberty Jail. *Experience* in this context suggests a refined nature, disposition, or temperament, not an accumulation of events. The experience we receive is a character that is approved of by God. Trials are suited in a marvelous way to increase the godliness of our character and personality. Mercy, forgiveness, compassion, longsuffering, kindness, gentleness, justice, benevolence are all attributes of Deity. We may ask ourselves what events of our lives are best calculated by their very nature to produce these qualities in a human soul. The answer is not difficult to discern. It is in the crucible of adversity that the gold of godliness is refined, molded, and shaped to perfection. Paul knew this and gloried in the assurance that the difficult trials of his life were making him, through his patience, a better man—a refined tool in the hands of the Lord.

Paul's formula concludes with the words, "and experience, hope: and hope maketh not ashamed; because the love of God is shed abroad in our hearts" (Romans 5:4-5). As our character continues to be refined through our tribulations and our patience, the hope that we are accepted of God becomes firmer and firmer, and we sense the Lord's approval and love. In his presence, our confidence grows and is heightened by the natural humility that comes with trial, unless we warp that humility into the false flower of self-inflicted martyrdom. Feeling our Father in Heaven's love and approval strengthens us with power to continue enduring the challenges, disappointments, and tribulations of life. As difficult as it is to believe, we may come to express gratitude for the hard times when we see them through time's lens and understand their tempering character and molding power. This does not lessen them while they are present; we would bid them be gone without even a parting wave, but from a distance their tutorial nature, if not their friendship, may be realized.

Not Worthy of Comparison

Paul also told the Saints in Rome, "I reckon that the sufferings of this present time are not worthy to be compared with the glory which shall be revealed in us" (Romans 8:18). That is a very strong statement. We can only believe it without reservation if we know that the man who uttered it had suffered to a high degree and also that he had an idea of future glory—otherwise, it is mere theological speculation or philosophical eyewash. Remember, Paul used the word *glory* in regard to tribulations. He gloried in them! That is an amazing assertion. How many of us glory in tribulation? We may trust Paul's witness, however. We do have some idea of both Paul's sufferings and also of his foreknowledge of the eternal worlds, for he wrote of both experiences to the Corinthian Saints, describing the hardships of his life in the following brief passage:

"In stripes above measure, in prisons more frequent, in deaths oft. Of the Jews five times received I forty stripes save one. Thrice was I beaten with rods, once was I stoned, thrice I suffered shipwreck, a night and a day I have been in the deep; in journeyings often, in perils of waters, in perils of robbers, in perils by mine own countrymen, in perils by the heathen, in perils in the city, in perils in the wilderness, in perils in the sea, in perils among false brethren; in weariness and painfulness, in watchings often, in hunger and thirst, in fastings often, in cold and nakedness" (2 Corinthians 11:23-27).

I think we can conclude without equivocation that Paul knew something of suffering and adversity. And in the very next chapter of 2 Corinthians, he assures us he also unequivocally knows something of the glory of the next world: "I will come to visions and revelations of the Lord. I knew a man in Christ above fourteen years ago, (whether in the body, I cannot tell; or whether out of the body, I cannot tell: God knoweth;) such an one caught up to the third heaven. And I knew such a man . . . how that he was caught up into paradise, and heard unspeakable words, which it is not lawful for a man to utter" (2 Corinthians 12:1-4). Though he does not state outright that the man he speaks of is himself, there is no question that is who he means.

Here we have a man who knew pain and had also seen the future glory in store for the faithful. With his grasp of those opposing realities, Paul still affirmed that we cannot compare the two: The glory surpasses the pain. In addition, Paul was given his own unique trial to endure. We do not know its nature, but he refers to it occasionally in his letters. It was in the context of both his pain and his knowledge of future glory that Paul wrote: "Lest I should be exalted above measure through the abundance of the revelations, there was given to me a thorn in the flesh." Notice that this persistent problem was given to Paul to "buffet" him lest he "should be exalted above measure." His knowledge of the humility his personal thorn was creating tempered its pain, but he still "besought the Lord thrice, that it might depart from me" (2 Corinthians 12:7-8).

Good—the good of humility, a humility that was in itself a catalyst for further revelation—came from Paul's thorn. We may think of this as we feel the worrisome annoyance and outright pain of our own thorns. They may have been placed, or allowed so that we may derive some greater good therefrom.

We have the hope of a greater glory, one not worthy of comparison to the pains of mortality. Because we do know somewhat concerning the horrific spread and intensity of human suffering, the glory that Paul saw when he was "caught up" should tell us something (2 Corinthians 12:4). Perhaps this is partially what Isaiah meant when he wrote of our inability to comprehend future blessedness: "For since the beginning of the world men have not heard, nor perceived by the ear, neither hath the eye seen, O God, beside thee, what he hath prepared for him that waiteth for him" (Isaiah 64:4). Perhaps we place too much emphasis on our present sufferings because we do not fully realize the promise of future rewards or the Lord's ability to add the vertical line that makes our present negative into a godly positive. The Lord once comforted the early Saints of this dispensation by saying, "Verily, verily, I say unto you, ye are little children, and ye have not as yet understood how great blessings the Father hath in his own hands and prepared for you; . . . be of good cheer, for I will lead you along. . . . The riches of eternity are yours" (D&C 78:17-18).

In his Epistle to the Ephesians, Paul indicated that God's ability to transform sorrow into good and to bless us beyond even the memory of pain "passeth knowledge." He prayed that we all "may be able to comprehend with all saints what is the breadth, and length, and depth, and height; and to know the love of Christ." Paul then assured the Ephesian Saints that God "is able to do exceeding abundantly above all that we ask or think" (Ephesians

3:18–20). Each one of us can ask or imagine a great deal that would make us happy and ensure eternal joy, but even our most robust imaginings cannot reach the dimensions of God's love. He will always exceed our highest dreams or aspirations. Good will come from adversity, and that good is beyond our very limited mortal capacity to reason. Let us continue to pray for the removal of our thorns, but if our prayer seems unheeded, may we hear the whisper of the Lord, "Peace, child. I am at work."

Forgetfulness and Fruitfulness in the Land of Affliction

Much of what we have spoken of tends toward an eternal view. If we are patient, in the eternities all will be made well and our realization of glory will so completely eclipse our past pains that they will be but a fleeting memory. With hindsight we will recognize their refining power. Thinking of this future may help to a degree, but what of the here and now? The scriptures testify that the good God intends to make from our suffering comes equally in mortality.

Joseph, the son of Israel who was sold by his brothers into Egypt and then falsely accused of immoral advances to Potiphar's wife, knew something of this truth. He too testifies that God can make all negatives positive and that the positives may come sooner than we had hoped.

Names are very important in the Old Testament. Often the name a parent gives a child carries the main theme or message of the surrounding story. This is true of the names *Isaac* and *Ishmael*, for example, which mean, respectively, "to rejoice," and "God hears."[1] It is certainly true also of Joseph's life. Here is a man who, like Paul, understood from experience the injustice of the world and the sufferings it inflicted. We are told that Joseph stood before

Pharaoh to interpret his dream when he was thirty years old. That was the turning point of his life. We are also told that he was seventeen when his problems with his brothers reached their crisis, and he was sold into Egypt. The adversities of his life lasted roughly thirteen years, yet at their conclusion he married Asenath, who bore him two sons, whom he named Manasseh and Ephraim. These names tell us something of Joseph's mind and soul after his years of bitterness.

"And Joseph called the name of the firstborn Manasseh: For God, said he, hath made me forget all my toil, and all my father's house" (Genesis 41:51). Manasseh means "forgetting."[2] "And the name of the second called he Ephraim: For God hath caused me to be fruitful in the land of my affliction" (Genesis 41:52). Ephraim means "fruitful."[3] The theme of Joseph's experiences is found in the names of his sons. God can cause us to forget all our toil and make us fruitful even in the land of our affliction. That is a remarkable truth and one the Lord wanted us to receive early in the scriptural record.

Joseph clearly understood the Lord's ability to draw good out of tribulation. It enabled him to freely forgive his brothers even as he tried to explain the principle to them. When Joseph, with tears, revealed his true identity, he said: "Now therefore be not grieved, nor angry with yourselves, that ye sold me hither: for God did send me before you to preserve life. . . . And God sent me before you to preserve you a posterity in the earth, and to save your lives by a great deliverance. So now it was not you that sent me hither, but God" (Genesis 45:5, 7-8). We understand, of course, that Joseph is being gracious to his brothers here; he is not saying that God inspired their actions. God did not send Joseph to Egypt; Joseph's brothers sold him there. But because of Joseph's humility and faithfulness, God changed the consequences of his jealous brothers' wicked actions into a positive, saving outcome. The forgetfulness and the fruitfulness Joseph felt when naming his sons arose out of his realization of what God had done for him in his affliction.

Despite Joseph's tears of forgiveness, his brothers' fears never entirely abated. After their reconciliation, Joseph brought his brothers' families and his father, Jacob, into Egypt to dwell. We are specifically told that Jacob lived in Egypt for seventeen years (see Genesis 47:28). When Jacob died, the brothers' fears resurfaced. They said, "Joseph will peradventure hate us, and certainly requite us all the evil which we did unto him" (Genesis 50:15). This happened forty years after their original sin. Guilt can be dreadful and not easily relinquished, even after forgiveness and years of normal relations. When Joseph learned of their anxiety, he calmed them with his forgiveness and love, explaining once again God's power in bringing goodness out of agony and evil: "Fear not: for am I in the place of God? But as for you, ye thought evil against me; but God meant it unto good, to bring to pass, as it is this day, to save much people alive" (Genesis 50:19-20). Joseph used the phrase "meant it unto good." We might choose a verb closer to the truth of the matter, certainly as it applies to us: God *brought* it to good.

Joseph is a perfect example of Paul's teaching. Paul encouraged us to be patient and to love God; then the changing of adversity to blessing could take place. For thirteen years Joseph endured in patience, faith, and love of God—his God did not fail him. Neither will he fail us.

"The Greatness of God"

Father Lehi named his two sons born in the wilderness Jacob and Joseph. Perhaps it is fitting, all things considered, that Lehi would teach this hope-inspiring principle to his son Jacob. In Lehi's view, the ability of God to transform suffering to glory, bitter to sweet, and darkness to light constituted his greatness. Lehi said to his young son: "And now, Jacob, I speak unto you: Thou art my first-born in the days of my tribulation in the wilderness. And behold, in thy childhood thou hast suffered afflictions and much sorrow, because of the rudeness of thy brethren" (2 Nephi 2:1).

I have often pondered that brief reference to the suffering of both Lehi and Jacob. Lehi calls his time in the wilderness the days of his tribulation, and we can only imagine what a child might suffer during those wanderings and the family conflicts that dominated their slow advance. Yet Lehi continues on a much brighter note: "Nevertheless, Jacob, my firstborn in the wilderness, thou knowest the greatness of God; and he shall consecrate thine afflictions for thy gain. Wherefore, thy soul shall be blessed" (2 Nephi 2:2–3).

What does the greatness of God consist of? I suppose there is no end of answers we could give for that question. But Lehi testifies that God's greatness consists of his ability to consecrate—an interesting word to use in this context—affliction to gain. *Consecrate* means to make holy. We make things holy by giving them to God. It is remarkable to think that among the things that we can give to God is our suffering and that in his hands all things become sanctified and adapted to their proper use. We are once again being taught the truth Paul taught the Romans and Joseph illustrated by naming his sons and forgiving his brothers. Lehi's words to his son Jacob seem to indicate that the positive that God will make from the negative "rudeness" Jacob endured as a child could be centered on his soul. God is in the business of developing souls. And as we have seen, affliction is a powerful tool in carving the soul into the image of God. Thus, affliction may be a blessing, though it is something we usually pray to avoid.

Lesson of Liberty Jail

Let us consider one final scriptural example of God's promise that he will make the negative in our lives positive. In words that echo Paul and Lehi, the Lord told the suffering and pleading Joseph Smith in Liberty Jail, "And if thou shouldst be cast into the pit, or into the hands of murderers, and the sentence of death passed upon thee; if thou be cast into the deep; if the billowing surge conspire against thee; if fierce winds become thine enemy; if the heavens gather blackness, and all the elements combine to hedge up the way; and above all, if the very jaws of hell shall gape open the mouth wide after thee, know thou, my son, that all these things shall give thee experience, and shall be for thy good" (D&C 122:7).

Some very interesting things are going on in this passage. First of all, the three main sources of pain and trial are listed. Adversity and affliction may come into our lives from the impersonal forces of nature; they may come from the evil dispositions of men and the injustices they often perpetrate; and they may come from the adversary himself—the gaping jaws of hell. Nature, humankind, and the adversary may come into all of our lives as affliction. These are the sources of human conflict. It bears mentioning that opposition from humankind may be of our own making, not only from the weaknesses, malice, or selfishness of others. We can be our own worst enemy, as the old saying goes.

The second striking thing about this passage is the Lord's use of the word *experience*. I cannot help but think he is alluding to Paul's words in Romans 5. Joseph Smith admired Paul and turned to his writings for encouragement numerous times. The context of both verses certainly allows us to make the connection. Remember that in Paul's epistle, *experience* suggests a character worthy of God's approval. As hard as our adversities may be to face, they will mold us into the divine image if we let them, for we can just as easily allow them to do the opposite. We can become bitter, angry, cruel, vengeful, faithless, despondent, despairing, broken, or defeatist, but we will largely choose those responses ourselves. Our afflictions—as difficult as they may be—are permitted by a wise Father in Heaven, who will turn them to his own divine purposes.

The Lord concludes his message of peace to Joseph with the striking words, "Therefore, hold on thy way . . . for God shall be with you forever and ever" (D&C 122:9). That is the essence of our challenge: heedless of the circumstances of our lives, we must hold on and stay true to the principles we have been taught. We must continue down the path believing that all good things, all desirable blessings, the fulfillment of all our deepest hopes lies along—and at the end of—our path. We need only proceed in the anticipation that all blessings will in time come to us. Ultimately, that is all that matters. And we have the Lord's promise that he will be with us and transform those sorrowful times to glory.

While we are in the throes and agonies of suffering, it is not easy to receive the comfort that God will consecrate these experiences to our redemption, but that is an essential truth God meant us to receive. His prophets placed it in multiple locations in the sacred texts so that we would not miss it and that we might understand by its frequent repetition how completely we may have faith in its consoling assurance.

C. S. Lewis understood this truth; he discovered it in the scriptures—as we may, if we search. I can think of no more fitting summary to this truth than that written by this English theologian and defender of Christianity: "'Ye cannot in your present state understand eternity. . . . But ye can get some likeness of it if you say that both good and evil, when they are full grown, become retrospective.

. . . All [this] earthly past will have been Heaven to those who are saved. . . . That is what mortals misunderstand. They say of some temporal suffering, "No future bliss can make up for it," not knowing that Heaven, once attained, will work backwards and turn even that agony into a glory. . . . The good man's past begins to change so that his forgiven sins and remembered sorrows take on the quality of Heaven. . . . And that is why, at the end of all things, when the sun rises here . . . the Blessed will say "We have never lived anywhere except in Heaven." . . . Ah, the Saved . . . what happens to them is best described as the opposite of a mirage. What seemed, when they entered it, to be the vale of misery turns out, when they look back, to have been a well; and where present experience saw only salt deserts, memory truthfully records that the pools were full of water.'"[4]

Prayers for Bodil

We have discussed God's bringing positives out of negatives as that truth relates to ourselves, but it is equally true that the good that God brings forth out of the crucible of suffering may also be directed toward others. He has promised that nothing can happen to us that he will not turn to his glory, but in his grand wisdom, that good may redound to the blessing of those we do not know. It may spread to generations yet unborn. As the Saints prepared for their westward journey, the Lord told them there would be hardships to endure. "If thou art sorrowful," he taught them, "call on the Lord thy God with supplication, that your souls may be joyful" (D&C 136:29). The prayers uttered by and in behalf of one single individual have haunted and inspired me every time I think of the great tragedy of the westward movement of the Saints—that of the Willie and Martin handcart companies.

I have had the opportunity of participating in several "trek" reenactments across the plains of Wyoming, sponsored by our stake leadership. We have pulled handcarts at Martin's Cove, waded through the Sweetwater River, climbed over Rocky Ridge, and camped under the stars at Rock Creek. All of these places were scenes of incredible suffering as the Saints of the Willie and Martin handcart companies struggled through the wind and snow of Wyoming blizzards.

There are so many stories that touch the heart that it is difficult to reduce them to a single example, but when I think of those painful moments in the snow, one individual always comes to mind. She presses upon my memory every time I walk the trail she walked, and when I stand at the spot where she was buried, her presence always seems very near. Her name is Bodil Mortensen. She was a young girl of nine who left Denmark for the promise of Zion. Her parents could not afford the journey for the whole family so she was sent ahead, entrusted to the care of the family of Jens Nielsen. The rest of the family would join her the following year. She endured the ordeal of Rocky Ridge, arriving alive but exhausted at the campground prepared by the rescuers at Rock Creek. There she was sent out to gather sagebrush for a fire. Having filled her arms with the needed brush she turned back to her tent, but exhaustion would have its way. Resting for a few moments against the wheel of a handcart, she fell asleep and froze to death. She was found in the morning, still clutching the wood she had gathered, leaning against the wheel. This image has such poignancy for me, but it is only one among many.

I have thought of the many prayers that were offered for Bodil and her companions. Surely loving and concerned parents were praying back in Denmark for the safe arrival of their little girl in Zion. Surely President Brigham Young was, in Salt Lake City, invoking the Lord to temper the elements and allow the wagons sent from the Salt

Lake Valley to bring back alive their precious cargo. But Bodil froze to death against a wagon wheel. I imagine Bodil herself prayed during those tedious days of snow and ice. I have wondered why God did not simply bump the jet stream a few hundred miles to the north and let a high pressure system bring needed warmth from the south. What an easy thing that would have been. He who calmed storms and multiplied bread, he who provided wine for a marriage feast could surely move a weather pattern a few hundred miles and allow Bodil to reach Salt Lake City in safety. Yet sacrifice, suffering, gives weight to testimony and pulls it deeper into the heart.

These thoughts turned in my mind as I pulled a handcart over Rocky Ridge one summer with my son. I had prayed that this experience would increase his faith and anchor him more firmly in the restored gospel. I looked at all the other young people trudging through the dust, handcarts bumping roughly against exposed rocks. I thought about the Lord contemplating the plight of the Willie and Martin handcart companies.

To the Lord all things are one great present. He was surely listening to the prayers of Bodil's parents back in Denmark, and Brigham Young's prayers, and the prayers of the handcart pioneers themselves. Then there were my prayers for my son and the prayers of thousands of other parents praying that the trek reenactment experience would enhance, change, develop, anchor, and create a deeper faith in their sons and daughters. How does one weigh such things in the balance?

God could see the immense good that would flow from the sacrifices, the painful, soul-wrenching sacrifices, from the memory that would stand forever of their struggles in the snow in 1856. So a decision was made, and the storms came, and Bodil died with her firewood carefully cradled in her arms. And now my son and I pulled in honor of her and her companions.

Sacrifice gives weight to faith and pulls it deep into the soul. Great and glorious good flowed from those bitter days in that unsheltered land—good for generations that followed and who yet follow and for any who contemplate the adversity that howled over the handcart pioneers' heads in the early fall storms. Jens Nielsen and his wife, Elsie, who were entrusted to take Bodil safe to Zion, lost their own six-year-old son, Niels, to that exhausting pull. He is buried with Bodil at Rock Creek. Years later Jens reflected on those trying times: "No person can describe it. It cannot be comprehended or understood by any human in this life, but only those who were called to pass through it."[5]

Jens used an interesting verb in his testimony. Were the handcart pioneers *called* to pass through suffering? Does God do that? However we answer that question, we know that their ordeal pulled testimony, with the weight of its collected miseries, into all of our hearts. Perhaps in God's wisdom that greater good could balance a frozen little girl and the prayers of her parents.

In the Lord's instructions to Brigham Young before the wagon trains and handcarts would cross Iowa, Nebraska, and Wyoming, he told of what would follow the sacrifices. "My people must be tried in all things, that they may be prepared to receive the glory that I have for them, even the glory of Zion" (D&C 136:31). Was the Lord referring to those early Saints themselves? Surely he was, but to a larger extent he was also referring to the glory that would continue down through the generations—the glory that would shine brighter because of the price others paid. When our limited sight fails to see good flowing from our own adversity, may the Lord give us eyes to see the goodness that will come to others through our example. In that vision we are instilled with enduring power.

—·∙∙∙·—

CHAPTER TWO

> Be merciful unto me, O Lord: for I cry
> unto thee daily. Rejoice the soul of thy servant: for
> unto thee, O Lord, do I lift up my soul. For thou,
> Lord, art good . . . and plenteous in mercy
> unto all them that call upon thee.
>
> *Psalm 86:3–5*

It Is Finished

"But a Small Moment"

Along with the truth that our Father in Heaven can bring goodness out of the adversities of our lives, there is, perhaps, no greater scriptural assurance than the knowledge that all trials will have an end. This is difficult to believe when we are in the grip of trials, for there are times in our lives when we do not believe we will ever be happy again, that our present distress will always continue—but no matter the cause, all pains come to an end. This is such an important concept that the scriptures emphasize it with frequency and intensity. They often teach it with a beauty of expression that carries great conviction. And we are also shown how to endure adversity while we wait for the promised relief.

One of the richest veins of truth is that found in the words of the Lord to Joseph Smith while he was in Liberty Jail. After Joseph's initial prayer, which begins Doctrine and Covenants 121, the Lord answers, "My son, peace be unto thy soul; thine adversity and thine afflictions shall be but a small moment" (v. 7). We have all probably had enough experience with life and the Lord's timing to realize that a small moment for the Lord may be quite a long one for us. His perspective is always focused on the eternal; ours is more short-sighted. One of the aspects of mortality with which we must deal is this: All of life itself may be "a small moment." The necessary thing to hold to is the confirming belief that at the end of the small moment, our adversity ends. We do not go into eternity—if that is the required limit of time—or on with our lives trailing the stinging dust of past storms. The wind ceases, the air clears, we draw a deep breath, and we walk on. One of the Psalms, attributed to Moses, speaks beautifully of the Lord's timing: "For a thousand years in thy sight are but as yesterday when it is past, and as a watch in the night. . . . So teach us to number our days, that we may apply our hearts unto wisdom" (Psalm 90:4, 12). We need wisdom when counting the days of our adversity.

Isaiah promised his people that there would come a time when God would "destroy" the veil of darkness "spread over all nations" (Isaiah 25:7). Enoch saw that the source of that darkness was the adversary, who rejoiced in the misery of mankind (see Moses 7:26). Isaiah continued his reassuring words: "He will swallow up death in victory; and the Lord God will wipe away tears from off all faces" (Isaiah 25:8). So powerful was this promise that John repeated it twice in the book of Revelation, adding intensity to it with his own unique emphasis. Speaking specifically of the souls who would come "out of great tribulation" during the turmoil of the sixth seal (our own time), John wrote, "They shall hunger no more, neither thirst any more; neither shall the sun light on them, nor any heat. For the Lamb which is in the midst of the throne shall feed them, and shall lead them unto living fountains of waters: and God shall wipe away all tears from their eyes" (Revelation 7:14, 16–17).

The sun and heat of this verse symbolize the oppositions and trials of life, and the hunger and thirst are not only our physical needs but also our emotional, spiritual, familial, and social needs, among others. In the concluding chapters of Revelation, John returns to Isaiah's promise, applying it to all people of all generations and all nations: "And God shall wipe away all tears from their eyes; and there shall be no more death, neither sorrow, nor crying, neither shall there be any more pain: for the former things are passed away" (Revelation 21:4).

There are tears of joy and tears of laughter, but most are tears of grief, tragedy, pain, and sorrow. We have shed them ourselves—tears from the anguish of physical pain endured in long, silent struggles; parental tears over a beloved but rebellious or apathetic child; spousal tears over conflict, rejection, divorce, or abandonment; bitter tears shed in guilt from repeated transgressions, addictions, or the consequences brought on by yielding to the forces of the natural man. Tears of loneliness drop from the eyes of the friendless and unloved; empathetic tears are tugged forth as we witness the cruelty and absurd brutality of human against human. And there are tears of separation when death comes, and the voices and faces we love are silenced and seen no more.

Yet the Lord tells us all this will end. He will wipe the tears from all faces. It is a powerful and beautiful image, because only those whom we deeply love and trust would be allowed to sweep a gentle hand across our face to wipe the tears away. So important is this truth that the very next verse contains God's direct command to write it so all may be assured of its fulfillment. "And he that sat upon the throne said, Behold, I make all things new. And he said unto me, Write: for these words are true and faithful" (Revelation 21:5).

In ancient times, great kings desired to give emphasis to their words. If they said it and wrote it, it would be done. I often think of Pharaoh's words in the movie *The Ten Commandments* when he pronounced "So let it be written! So let it be done!" It is in the spirit of confirming confidence that the Lord tells us the tears will be swept away: "Write: for these words are true and faithful." This is a truth the Lord wishes all mankind to receive. It is the promise of the King of Kings, and there is no higher authority than his. No one need doubt the personal, individual fulfillment of the promise. The tears will be gone!

The Last Words of Jesus

Some of the most profound lessons of the scriptures are contained in the brief but poignant words Jesus uttered from the cross. There is a sermon in each, but let us focus on Jesus' words when he said, "It is finished" (John 19:30). I see a number of meanings in these words. He had finished the bitter cup, the cup of trembling, right down to the last taste of vinegar on his lips, offered mockingly in response to his request "I thirst" (John 19:28). He had completed his mission, his Father's will; the grand moment in the Father's plan of mercy and happiness had been accomplished. But that grand moment also included his suffering. No other throughout the long ages of man has ever—nor will ever—suffer to the degree he did, yet there came a time in that suffering when he could say, "It is finished." It was finished, and that will likewise be true of each human soul. No matter what we have suffered, are now suffering, or may yet suffer, there will come a time when we will all echo his words: "It is finished!" Our tears will be changed, and though they will continue to flow, they will be tears of relief, tears of gratitude, tears of joy. The former things will have passed away.

That passing away will be so complete and the rejoicing so full that we will not remember, save for the lessons we have learned, our past pain. Isaiah, who was specifically enjoined to speak words of comfort to the people, recorded the Lord's words: "For, behold, I create new heavens and a new earth: and the former shall not be remembered, nor come into mind. But be ye glad and rejoice" (Isaiah 65:17–18).

Turn Outward

Our challenge, then, is to endure our small moment of suffering until the promised consummation, but the challenge comprises more than just endurance. The Lord specifically told Joseph he was to "endure it well" (D&C 121:8). There are times when I say to the Lord, "I think I can endure, but must I endure it well? Cannot I endure it with bitter tears, complaints, and worrying cries? Why must that word *well* be included in the mix?"

What can the scriptures teach us about enduring our adversity well? The scriptures do not leave us friendless in answering that question. It is one of the great questions of life. Let us see what aid they offer.

How did Jesus, himself, endure his hour? The answer is easily identifiable, at least in one element of his endurance. He turned outward! He focused his heart on others. As Jesus approached the last days and hours of his life, he said something to "certain Greeks" brought to him by Philip, which allows us to see deep into the heart of our Savior. John did not record what question they asked, but we have the Savior's response. "And Jesus answered them, saying, The hour is come. . . . *Now is my soul troubled; and what shall I say?*

Father, save me from this hour: but for this cause came I unto this hour" (John 12:20, 23, 27; emphasis added).

Here is one who knows the path before him, knows it will require great sacrifice of him, great agony, and yet he must walk it, however much he would like the Father to delay the end or remove his burden altogether. In the prayer of Gethsemane his anguished heart will humbly, beseechingly, make the request.

As Jesus drew those faithful few disciples around him in the final moments of peace at the Last Supper and looked at their faces, one face in particular troubled him again. After washing the feet of his disciples, who were still concerned about their places of prominence in the kingdom, Jesus said, "He that receiveth me receiveth him that sent me. When Jesus had thus said, *he was troubled in spirit,* and testified, and said, Verily, verily, I say unto you, that one of you shall betray me" (John 13:20-21; emphasis added).

I emphasize the word *troubled* because we will see it again in John's record of the Last Supper. As we gaze upon this scene in the imagination of our thoughts, can we begin to plumb the depths of the Savior's heart at this moment? What does he know as he looks into the faces of those he has loved and taught? He knows that Judas will betray him for a few pieces of silver. He also knows the despair that betrayal will bring upon the man he called friend, and perhaps he can see Judas's body hanging lifeless, whose deep remorse held no mercy for himself. That would certainly have touched the center of his mercies. He knows as he looks at Peter that Peter, the rock, before the rooster crows twice will deny that he even knows Jesus and will deny him three times. He knows that the other disciples will flee, for he tells them, "All ye shall be offended because of me this night: for it is written, I will smite the shepherd, and the sheep of the flock shall be scattered abroad" (Matthew 26:31).

Jesus knows that within the next few hours he will carry the burden of earth's suffering, its wickedness, and its subsequent misery upon himself. He knows he will be mocked, spat upon, scourged, and finally crucified. All this he has known from before his ministry, for he has read and understood the prophecies and the Psalms. He has studied these from his youth and has communed deeply with his Father and knows his will. If ever there was a soul from the beginning of time who needed comfort and reassurance, it was Jesus at this time. Yet as we read the account of the Last Supper and the events of his trials, condemnation, and death, we become acquainted with a marvelous truth. Who comforts whom?

"Let Not Your Heart Be Troubled"

Some of the most beautiful statements of Jesus Christ are contained in his comforting words to the disciples during the Last Supper. He senses their confusion and sadness, their growing apprehension that something is going to happen to their Lord. As Jesus looks at their anxious faces, he offers the following consolation. It is important that we notice the deep irony of Jesus' use of the word *troubled:*

"*Let not your heart be troubled:* ye believe in God, believe also in me. In my Father's house are many mansions: if it were not so, I would have told you. I go to prepare a place for you. And if I go and prepare a place for you, I will come again, and receive you unto myself; that where I am, there ye may be also" (John 14:1–3; emphasis added).

A little later Jesus says, "Peace I leave with you, my peace I give unto you: not as the world giveth, give I unto you. *Let not your heart be troubled,* neither let it be afraid" (John 14:27; emphasis added).

At the final moments before Gethsemane, Jesus once again offers his comforting assurances: "In the world ye shall have tribulation: but be of good cheer; I have overcome the world" (John 16:33).

These and other verses we could examine must all be read against the backdrop of Jesus' own troubled heart if we are to receive the full import of their message and guidance when we face similar times of adversity and trouble. His lesson of looking outward when our heart cries to look inward to our own pains continues throughout the final hours of the Savior's mortal life. Consider the import of these statements and actions: When the arresting party took him after his agony in Gethsemane, "Jesus answered, I have told you that I am he; if therefore ye seek me, let these go their way" (John 18:8). To Pilate, who desired to free Jesus and was troubled both by his own conscience and his wife's dream, Jesus said, "Thou couldest have no power at all against me, except it were given thee from above: therefore he that delivered me unto thee hath the greater sin" (John 19:11). This is not a release from judicial and moral responsibility but a soft understanding of Pilate's heart and the dilemma he was facing.

Even on the cross, despite his own agony, the Lord continued to offer comfort to others. To his mother, Mary, who was standing at the foot of the cross with John, he said, "Woman, behold thy son! Then saith he to the disciple, Behold thy mother!" (John 19:26–27). To the dying thief hanging next to him: "Verily I say unto thee, To day shalt thou be with me in paradise" (Luke 23:43). To the soldiers who drove the nails into his flesh, gambled for his robe, and mocked him with vinegar: "Father, forgive them; for they know not what they do" (Luke 23:34). Even after his suffering had ended, we see him at the moment of his Resurrection tenderly calling Mary's name at the Garden Tomb, spending a brief moment to assuage her fears rather than immediately ascending to his Father.

The dominant message of the last hours of our Savior's life is, When you need comfort, comfort others. Turn your focus outward, and a peace will penetrate the inward emptiness that a more deliberate effort will fail to achieve.

Letters from Rome

Though Jesus is the great example of this principle, it is not difficult to see evidence of it elsewhere in the scriptures. A few examples of emphasizing the importance of looking outward might prove helpful. Many of the epistles of Paul—for example, Galatians, Ephesians, Philippians, Colossians, 2 Timothy, and Philemon—were all written from Rome while Paul was in prison awaiting trial before Caesar. They are filled with solicitous statements concerning the welfare of his converts. We would be hard-pressed to find any self-pity or distress over his own condition anywhere in Paul's writings. All his words were directed to the spiritual welfare of the churches. To the Galatians he wrote: "Let us not be weary in well doing: for in due season we shall reap, if we faint not. As we have therefore opportunity, let us do good unto all men" (Galatians 6:9-10). To the Saints in Philippi, Paul expressed his positive view of life and hoped his own imprisonment would be an inspiration to all who might face their own trials: "Every where and in all things I am instructed both to be full and to be hungry, both to abound and to suffer need. I can do all things through Christ which strengtheneth me" (Philippians 4:12-13).

Perhaps Paul's attitude during his imprisonment can best be seen in the tiny Epistle to Philemon which begins with the words,

"Paul, a prisoner . . ." The rest of the epistle centers on a runaway slave named "Onesimus, whom I have begotten in my bonds." Paul beseeches his friend Philemon to forgive and accept his former slave and to "receive him as myself. If he hath wronged thee, or oweth thee ought, put that on mine account." Paul was so concerned with the difficult state of Onesimus that he wrote the letter with his own hand instead of relying on a scribe, as was his custom. "I Paul have written it with mine own hand. . . . Yea, brother, let me have joy of thee in the Lord" (Philemon 1:1, 10, 17-20).

We could also examine the setting of the Revelation of John, written while he was a prisoner on the tiny, barren island of Patmos. Like Paul's epistles, Revelation, which was John's epistle to the Saints of Asia, also contains concern for the spiritual welfare of the Saints. There is no evidence of John's dissatisfaction with his lot.

A third example may be helpful. When Joseph was imprisoned due to the false accusations of Potiphar's wife, we see evidence of his concern for his fellow prisoners. He, too, turned outward. When the chief butler and baker were disturbed by their dreams, they did not go to Joseph for help; noticing their sorrow, he went to them. "And Joseph came in unto them in the morning, and looked upon them, and, behold, they were sad. And he asked Pharaoh's officers that were with him in the ward of his lord's house, saying, Wherefore look ye so sadly to day?" (Genesis 40:6-7). Joseph then told them that the interpretation of dreams belongs to God and that he would grant them understanding.

It is not easy to turn outward when our instinct tells us to concentrate on our own situation. Yet there is a release offered in focusing on the troubles of others, in searching for those who need a sympathetic touch, in giving solace to those in pain, for in so doing, we find that many of our own needs are met, and we will receive the Lord's assurance that we are enduring well.

The scriptures give us more truths about enduring well; other examples are instructive, and we shall examine them as we continue through the Lord's books. Before doing so, however, we turn to a Hindu parable that may also be helpful as well as enlightening.

The Wishing Tree

God speaks to man through numerous voices. Those who cannot hear the voice of prophets may hear the voice of a poet, a playwright, a sage, or a philosopher. I have found his voice in many places. I have long loved a Hindu parable about a tree that granted anything one wished for. It is highly instructive and may help amplify the principle of turning outward.

The story begins in a poor village in India, where children are playing with the rough toys of a rural society, dolls made from sticks and marbles made from pebbles. An uncle visits them from the city and, observing their activities, tells them they can have much more. Don't they realize that just outside their village is a wishing tree? The Hindus call the tree Kalpataru, or Kalpavriksha. It is the world tree. As Christians, we might consider it the Tree of the Knowledge of Good and Evil.

"Don't stay here with your simple toys," their uncle tells them. "Go outside and wish! The tree will give you all you ask for."

The children rush outside. At first they are somewhat skeptical, but as they gather around the tree and begin to make wishes they discover that the uncle is right. The tree gives whatever they desire—the desire is sufficient to bring it to pass. What do they wish for? At first they wish for sweets and toys, the desires of children. They receive all they desire, but the tree brings forth a surprise. The children also receive the opposite of their wish. No wish fulfilled in life comes alone; it brings its opposite.

Does not our own name for such a tree suggest the same truth? Did not Lehi teach us that?

So the children get stomachaches from the sweets and boredom from the toys. They wish again, for bigger and grander toys, and they receive, along with the toys, greater and deeper boredom. Perhaps you know someone who continually wishes for the newest toys the market can provide. Does not the opposite ultimately materialize? Boredom, ennui, dissatisfaction, and eventually more wishing? Perhaps we are all children wishing under the tree, our desires stoked and fired by the latest advertising campaign peddling its fruits.

Something must be wrong, the children think. They are obtaining their desires, but happiness is still somehow elusive. They grow older under the tree and become young men and women—adults! They are mature now and know the things they really want. "Sweets and toys—of course they cannot satisfy! There are other fruits much more desirable! We are no longer children! We know now what to wish for." Their wishing takes on a more serious tone. They now wish for the four fruits that hang on the tree: pleasure, fame, wealth, and power. These now become the focus of their desires and subsequent wishing. They obtain all they wish for. The tree always delivers, but the ever-present opposite also appears. They have anxiety, frustration, worry, deceit, contention, adversity, suffering, war, despair, disillusionment, and all the other consequences of wanting the four fruits of the tree—the sad litany of mankind's search for fulfillment. Can happiness really result in desires centered on self?

Time marches onward, and the children grow old under the tree. Now they divide into three groups. The first says, "What a terrible world this is! Nothing is good! Nothing is real or lasting! Who would create such a world?" These are fools, who have learned nothing from life. The second group says, "The problem is with our wishing. We made the wrong wishes! We just need to turn to the tree and wish for the right things!" These are even greater fools. The third group no longer wants anything to do with this inadequate, horrible world. "If this is the way life is," they say, "we just wish to die." They have reached the state of Macbeth, who at the end of Shakespeare's play gives his famous soliloquy upon hearing of his wife's death:

> *Life's but a walking shadow,*
> *A poor player that struts and frets*
> *His hour upon the stage,*
> *And then is heard no more.*
> *It is a tale told by an idiot,*
> *Full of sound and fury,*
> *Signifying nothing.*[1]

Of course the tree grants them their wish, and it also gives them the opposite—rebirth. Life will be lived all over again. According to Hindu and Buddhist religious belief, we are all reborn until we learn the essential truth about life, the truth that liberates us, the truth that frees one from the tree and cuts through its roots. What a dilemma these children end up facing.

The whole time a solitary child has watched his companions wishing under the tree. He is lame and could not rush out when the uncle told them of the wishing tree. He has been sitting in a nearby hut witnessing his friends and the Kalpataru existence they are living. He watches the sweets and the stomachaches. He watches the toys and the boredom. He watches them obtain the four fruits and receive anxiety, frustration, sickness, suffering, contention. He watches them reach their final decisions and wishes at the twilight of life. They are suffering, and yet they continue to make wishes that the tree dutifully grants along with the ever-present opposites.

The parable now reaches its climax and the answer. As the lame child watches his fellow children, a deep, spontaneous, and continuous wave of compassion sweeps through him, overwhelms him, fills every part of him, and in the power of this selfless sympathy for his friends, he forgets to wish for himself. The flame of selfish desire is extinguished, and all emotion, all focus, is centered outward. He has cut through the roots of the tree and is liberated. He has no wishes, and for him the tree is powerless.

That is the parable. Christian theology would say that the lame child has immersed himself in charity, true charity, which "seeketh not her own" and without which we are "nothing" (Moroni 7:45-46). Yet even charity is an inadequate word for the deep swell of compassion the parable demands. For the Hindu and the Buddhist, release from suffering comes with letting go, blowing out, or extinguishing all selfish desires. This is what the Buddhists call Nirvana. One cannot suffer when all thought is compassionately directed to others. This must come naturally, or as the tellers of the story say, "You cannot remember not to wish!" The gush of compassion must come instinctively, purely, artlessly, without preconception. It is a state of release, a freedom few know.

But Jesus knew! And it carried him through Gethsemane, through Calvary!

—∿—

CHAPTER THREE

Let us labor diligently; . . . for we have a
labor to perform whilst in this tabernacle of clay.

Moroni 9:6

UNDER THE JUNIPER TREE

"What Doest Thou Here, Elijah?"

There is a certain type of solace to be gained when we realize that the greatest of God's prophets have been so discouraged with the adversities of life that they wished to be released, not just from their calling but from mortality. How does the Lord lift his prophets out of these depths? Is there counsel for us in watching the Lord encourage men like Moses, Joshua, or Elijah? Let us see.

A high point in the prophet Elijah's ministry was his confrontation with the priests of Baal at Mount Carmel. Due in great part to the influence of Jezebel, the kingdom of Israel was enmeshed in the worship of false gods, Baal being the chief one. Because Baal was a god of rain and because Moses had promised the children of Israel that Jehovah would give them rain according to the seasons, an action that would likely convince the people to worship the true God was to ask God to shut the heavens. In other words, if the Israelites

WHAT THE SCRIPTURES TEACH US ABOUT ADVERSITY

were going to worship a false rain god, ask the true God to stop the rain. At the end of the three-and-a-half-year famine, Elijah challenged the priests of Baal to a demonstration of their power. Both Elijah and the priests of Baal would offer sacrifices to their respective gods, and the god who could send fire (lightning) from heaven with its subsequent rain would, obviously, be the true God. Elijah's faith in Jehovah was repaid, and all went as he had hoped. The failure of Jezebel's priests and the dramatic success of Elijah caused the people to say, "The Lord, he is the God; the Lord, he is the God" (1 Kings 18:39).

Elijah's success seemed short-lived, however. Soon afterward, Jezebel threatened Elijah's life, and he fled his homeland for the wilderness of Horeb (another name for Sinai). Apparently Elijah was not confident that the people would take his side against the chief worshiper of Baal.

The account of Elijah's flight in 1 Kings leaves no doubt of the depression, frustration, and discouragement of one of the Old Testament's most powerful prophets. "He himself went a day's journey into the wilderness, and came and sat down under a juniper tree: and he requested for himself that he might die; and said, It is enough; now, O Lord, take away my life; for I am not better than my fathers" (1 Kings 19:4). His fathers had not been successful in keeping the people constant in their worship of Jehovah, and now, in his mind, he had failed also.

There is something familiar about Elijah sitting disconsolately underneath the juniper tree. Metaphorically speaking, we have all camped there from time to time, possibly yielding to the temptation to stay there longer than is needful or healthy. Elijah went to sleep and awoke to a meal prepared by an angel to strengthen him. "And he did eat and drink, and laid him down again" (1 Kings 19:6). It is sometimes very difficult to leave the shade of our self-created junipers, but even while we're there, the Lord is solicitous of us, attentive to our needs, and nourishing. There should be no guilt in seeking the shade of the juniper, but how long do we stay there, and how do we face the heat of the sun again?

Once again the angel touched Elijah to awaken him from sleep for another meal. This time, after receiving refreshment, Elijah continued on to "Horeb the mount of God" (1 Kings 19:8). An enlightening conversation awaited him there.

At Mount Horeb, Elijah exchanged the juniper tree for a cave. This time, however, the Lord himself arouses Elijah to action. He asks him a simple question, "What doest thou here, Elijah?" Given an opportunity to get out all his frustration and disappointment, Elijah answers, "I have been very jealous for the Lord God of hosts: for the children of Israel have forsaken thy covenant, thrown down thine altars, and slain thy prophets with the sword; and I, even I only, am left; and they seek my life, to take it away" (1 Kings 19:9–10).

There is a subtle suggestion in the Lord's question. I am sure it was asked with solicitude and concern and in an engaging and loving tone, but I sense there is also just a hint of an answer in the very question itself: Should you be here, Elijah? Is there not a better place to be than in the cave or under the juniper?

There followed three impressive demonstrations of the Lord's power in a great wind, an earthquake, and a fire. Then a "still small voice" spoke and asked the question once again. "What doest thou here, Elijah?" (1 Kings 19:12–13). Elijah answered in the same words he had spoken previously.

The repetition of the question is intriguing. Is there a hint in the repetition, a hint that Elijah is not heeding in his eagerness to pour out his present disenchantment with being the Lord's spokesman?

Within the compass of the Lord's next two words we find a life-sustaining principle to aid us when we find ourselves in a similar position—in the juniper tree or cave moments of our lives: "Go, return" (1 Kings 19:15). The Lord then asks Elijah to take several actions with respect to the apostasy in Israel under Jezebel's rule, but it would probably not matter a great deal what the Lord asked Elijah to do. The important thing is that he take action. When we are discouraged, ready to give up—even to the degree of Elijah's wishing his life were over—the Lord tells us to go to work. We return to the world from our cave or our juniper tree. When we or others are facing life's adversities, one of the most helpful suggestions we can give or receive is just this: Act. Accomplish something. Anything is better than lying under a juniper tree or waiting in a cave. The very reality of achievement, no matter how small, may be the critical first step forward. The Lord gave Elijah three things to do: choose a new king of Syria, select a new king of Israel, and anoint Elisha as his own successor. This last instruction particularly would be helpful to Elijah as he trained and prepared the next prophet.

We will return to his story soon, for there is one more relevant truth to be gleaned from it about facing discouragement, but for now let us add insight to Elijah's lesson by exploring a time in the life of Moses when he too wished to die.

"It Is Too Heavy for Me"

Moses was surely a prophet who knew something of discouragement and despair. Time and time again his people challenged his leadership, questioned his wisdom, rebelled against God, and desired to return to Egypt and bondage, preferring it to all that Moses and the Lord desired to give them. As we have seen with Elijah, at one time in the wilderness Moses had had enough. Unfortunately, when you are a prophet and want to be released from your calling, that release is death. Even so, Moses favored that to continuing to lead the people.

During their wandering in the wilderness, the people wanted more variety in their diet. Manna was just not sufficient. "We remember the fish, which we did eat in Egypt freely; the cucumbers, and the melons, and the leeks, and the onions, and the garlick: but now our soul is dried away: there is nothing at all, beside this manna, before our eyes" (Numbers 11:5-6). Their murmuring was too much this time, and Moses cried to the Lord in frustration bordering on bitterness:

"Wherefore hast thou afflicted thy servant? and wherefore have I not found favour in thy sight, that thou layest the burden of all this people upon me? Have I conceived all this people? have I begotten them, that thou shouldest say unto me, Carry them in thy bosom, as a nursing father beareth the sucking child, unto the land which thou swarest unto their fathers? . . . I am not able to bear all this people alone, because it is too heavy for me. And if thou deal thus with me, kill me, I pray thee, out of hand, if I have found favour in thy sight; and let me not see my wretchedness" (Numbers 11:11-15).

As he did with Elijah, the Lord gives Moses something to do. "Gather unto me seventy men of the elders of Israel, whom thou knowest. . . . I will take of the spirit which is upon thee, and will put it upon them; and they shall bear the burden of the people with thee, that thou bear it not thyself alone" (Numbers 11:16-17). With his knowledge of the leaders of the people, Moses was to choose seventy who would help him in administering to the needs of the people. These men he brought to the tabernacle, and God laid some of the burden on them. In addition the Lord caused flocks of quail to fly into the camp. In the Israelites' eagerness and greed, however, they killed far more quail than they could consume and did not properly care for the meat. Disease spread through the camp.

The story is less important as an illustration of another rebellion by the children of Israel than it is as an illustration of Moses' fatigue. Even the greatest men and women encounter and deal with deep discouragement and despair. The Lord listens to their complaints—and there is no question that both Elijah and Moses complained—and then gives them something to do to help pull them through their tough times. Maybe, as with us, there is also a simple relief in just telling someone our feelings of doubt and discouragement. God has a good listening ear.

"Get Thee Up"

One more example might be useful. I love this particular response from the Lord because it has a touch of compelling irony and humor to it. Joshua has just won the battle at Jericho and sent a small army to the city of Ai to conquer it. Previous to the victory at Jericho, the Lord forbade anyone to take spoils from the city, but a man named Achan disobeyed and hid some money and cloth under his tent. Because of Achan's disobedience, the Lord allows the men sent to fight at Ai to suffer defeat. The Lord wanted the people to realize that what they did, and how they acted, had an effect on others, hence the disaster at Ai. The idea that we are only hurting ourselves with our decisions is a falsehood hatched in hell by the adversary, who wants us to think we can do what we want because "It's my life, and I am only hurting myself." The defeat at Ai disheartens all of Israel, and Joshua is deeply distressed.

Joshua tears his clothes and falls to the earth in prayer. "Alas, O Lord God, wherefore hast thou at all brought this people over Jordan, to deliver us into the hand of the Amorites, to destroy us? would to God we had been content, and dwelt on the other side Jordan!" (Joshua 7:6-7). We can hear his despair and distress. Joshua, the great warrior who as a spy years earlier had said of the Canaanites, "they are bread for us" (Numbers 14:9), wonders if it all will be worth it. Wouldn't it be easier to be content with living on the other side of the Jordan in a land already conquered during Moses' leadership? "O Lord, what shall I say, when Israel turneth their backs before their enemies! For the Canaanites and all the inhabitants of the land shall hear of it, and shall environ us round, and cut off our name from the earth: and what wilt thou do unto thy great name?" (Joshua 7:8-9).

Joshua uses interesting tactics in his conversation with the Lord. One thing we notice frequently with these men is how open they are in their prayers. They do not hold back their feelings in the least. That is refreshing for us to know, and we will discuss this later. Paraphrased, Joshua is saying, Certainly, Lord, you will want to help us for your own name's sake. We are fighting under your banner; how can you let us lose?

Notice the Lord's response: "And the Lord said unto Joshua, Get thee up; wherefore liest thou thus upon thy face? Israel hath sinned. . . . Up, sanctify the people" (Joshua 7:10-11, 13). The Lord's answer to Joshua, "Get thee up," is reminiscent of his answer to Elijah, "What doest thou here?" Paraphrased again, the Lord is saying, This is not a time to lie on your face commiserating with me—get up and tend to your people.

I am sure this instruction was stated as gently as possible, yet we detect a touch of irony that makes the verse so very wonderful. And the Lord gives Joshua something to do that will lead to solving the problem.

Even great leaders face times of debilitating adversity, times of deep distress, times they want to give up, complain to the Lord, or just sit under a juniper tree. They are human. We can relate to them. Our own challenging times become more bearable when we know that even the greatest of God's children act and feel as we do sometimes. What they teach us—what the Lord teaches us, and them—is the need to be up and moving, to act, to find something positive to do. Begin to solve the problem even if, as in each of the cases we've discussed, you do not know how everything is going to turn out. A spark of faith may be all that is necessary to "get thee up."

CHAPTER FOUR

—꿈—

I am distressed for thee, my brother Jonathan:
very pleasant hast thou been unto me: thy love to
me was wonderful, passing the love of women.

2 Samuel 1:26

THY FRIENDS DO STAND BY THEE

Burdens Made Bearable

We gain another comforting truth from the accounts of Moses and Elijah as they learn how to endure adversity well. Both men are assured they are not alone in the opposition they are facing. Elijah, who told the Lord, "I, even I only, am *left*," was assured, "Yet I have *left* me seven thousand in Israel, all the knees which have not bowed unto Baal, and every mouth which hath not kissed him" (1 Kings 19:14, 18; emphasis added). Notice the power that is instilled into the story by the Lord's repetition of Elijah's word *left*.

In the case of Moses, who felt his burden was "too heavy" (Numbers 11:14), the Lord had him call seventy other men to share the load. There followed an outpouring of the Spirit on these men that caused Moses to remark, "Would God that all the Lord's people were prophets, and that the Lord would put his spirit upon them!" (Numbers 11:29).

The scriptures share with us many other stories of burdens made bearable because more than one pair of shoulders helped with the load. The weeping Hannah, disconsolate over her barrenness, was comforted by a sympathetic husband, who offered her his own love as a compensating balance. "Hannah," he said, "why weepest thou? and why eatest thou not? and why is thy heart grieved? am not I better to thee than ten sons?" (1 Samuel 1:8–9). Though Elkanah's sympathy could not fill the space of desired children, Hannah accepted his love and ended her fast.

There are few examples of sustaining friendship in all literature more beautiful than that between David and Jonathan, a son of Saul. David acknowledged that love in his lament over Jonathan: "Very pleasant has thou been unto me: thy love to me was wonderful, passing the love of women" (2 Samuel 1:26). David, hunted relentlessly by Saul, turned to Jonathan time and time again and never failed to receive needed support, for "Jonathan loved him as his own soul" (1 Samuel 18:1). Fearing for his life as "Saul sought him every day," and often in distress, David was succored as "Jonathan Saul's son arose, and went to David into the wood, and strengthened his hand in God" (1 Samuel 23:14, 16).

That last phrase is such a worthy one! It acknowledges that our own strength is rarely sufficient, and those who face adversity can turn to One who does have what is needed. Isaiah assured his people that the God who "measured the waters in the hollow of his hand . . . and weighed the mountains in scales, and . . . sitteth upon the circle of the earth . . . giveth power to the faint; and to them that have no might he increaseth strength" (Isaiah 40:12, 22, 29). Notice that Isaiah does not indicate the Lord will remove the burdens life may place upon us; rather he increases our ability to carry them. He is the best of all possible friends. Often his strengthening power is manifested by the presence of a friend or family member in the mold of a Jonathan or an Elkanah.

"Warm Hearts and Friendly Hands"

There is no question that sharing our burdens with others, knowing that others care and understand our loads, is comforting and strengthening. There is power in friendship in particular. The Lord used this idea to help alleviate Joseph Smith's suffering and low spirits when he was in Liberty Jail. The Prophet's prayer at the commencement of Doctrine and Covenants 121 has the same intensity and complaint we hear in Elijah's, Moses', Joshua's, and Hannah's prayers: "O God, where art thou? . . . How long shall thy hand be stayed?" (D&C 121:1–2).

"Thy friends do stand by thee," the Lord replied, "and they shall hail thee again with warm hearts and friendly hands" (D&C 121:9). What a wonderful phrase to hang truth on—"warm hearts and friendly hands"! It is followed by a reference to Job, whose story we will examine later. Often what we need most—and what the Lord provides—when we face adversity is the strength of warm hearts and friendly hands. We look for our Jonathan, our Elkanah. It is also what we must offer when others, especially those we love, face the sorrows and blows of life.

A unique power is instilled in the Lord's words to Joseph, power which we can receive by exploring the full context of Joseph's experiences in Liberty Jail. Section 121 is part of a letter Joseph wrote from Liberty to the Saints gathering in Illinois. We do not have the complete letter in the Doctrine and Covenants, but knowing the missing parts adds insight to those that are canonized as scripture. Section 121 begins with Joseph's prayer of anguish, a prayer much in the spirit of those of Elijah, Moses, and Joshua, as we have seen. The prayer ends in verse 6, and in verse 7 begins the Lord's comforting reply. In the original letter Joseph tells of something that happened between his prayer and the Lord's response. That event teaches us a great truth about facing and enduring adversity.

"We Received Some Letters"

Joseph writes: "We received some letters last evening—one from Emma, one from Don C. Smith, and one from Bishop Partridge—all breathing a kind and consoling spirit. . . . When we read those letters they were to our souls as the gentle air is refreshing. . . . Those who have not been enclosed in the walls of prison . . . can have but little idea how sweet the voice of a friend is; one token of friendship from any source whatever awakens and calls into action every sympathetic feeling. . . . it moves the mind backward and forward, from one thing to another, until finally all enmity . . . and past differences, misunderstandings and mismanagements are slain victorious at the feet of hope; and when the heart is sufficiently contrite, then the voice of inspiration steals along and whispers, [My son, peace be unto thy soul]."[1]

In the case of Joseph Smith, we might conclude that the Lord wanted to offer comfort, but the emotional turmoil of his soul became a barrier until the tokens of friendship put him in a state of mind that he could receive the Lord's relieving message of hope. In our need, we might shout down the whispers of heaven and compound our own grief by delaying counsel and instruction that could bring it to a speedier end. Ironically, our very need for the soothing voice of God might prevent it from coming. This is where friends and family can provide their perhaps most valuable assistance. Their offers of sympathy, understanding, and listening ears may put us in a state of both mind and soul where we can hear God's persistent, but not forced, voice.

In an earlier and less-known letter from Liberty Jail written to Mrs. Norman Bull, Joseph also mentions the power of friends in assuaging adversity. It is in many ways a masterpiece on adversity because it contains so many of the truths we have discussed thus far. Joseph begins with, "My heart rejoices at the friendship you manifest in requesting to have a conversation with us." Conversations in the jail were very restricted because of the jailer's fear that friends might smuggle tools to the prisoners to help them escape. Joseph, however, appreciates and lauds her friendship; her very offer and desires to assist were a sufficient blessing. "Oh, what joy it would be to us to see our friends! It would have gladdened my heart to have had the privilege of conversing with you. . . . I want . . . you to know that I am your true friend. I was glad to see you. No tongue can tell what inexpressible joy it gives a man, after having been enclosed in the walls of a prison for five months, to see the face of one who has been a friend."

Joseph has learned something from the solicitations of his friends, and he continues with wonderful words describing the effect we can have on one another during times of trial. "It seems to me that my heart will always be more tender after this than ever it was before." Then Joseph directs his comments and emotions to the suffering Saints, a message that testifies to the truth of the need to turn outward when we ourselves are surrounded by adversity. "My heart bleeds continually when I contemplate the distress of the Church. O, that I could be with them! I would not shrink at toil and hardship to render them comfort and consolation."

Quoting Paul's words to the Romans, Joseph emphasizes another source of strength when facing the sorrows of mortality—the knowledge that everything will be turned into a blessing in the wisdom and greatness of God. Joseph's realization of this precedes the Lord's promise to him, which is written in the later letter and which we have in Doctrine and Covenants 121 through 123. "Trials will only give us the knowledge necessary to understand the minds of the ancients. For my part, I think I never could have felt as I now do, if I had not suffered the wrongs that I have suffered. All things shall work together for good to them that love God." Joseph then encourages Mrs. Bull not to "have any feelings of enmity towards any son or daughter of Adam" and closes the letter.[2] Friends are powerful allies in the adversities of life. These letters give added meaning to the Lord's words to the Prophet that "thy friends do stand by thee" (D&C 121:9).

"Watch with Me"

In the final hours of the Savior's life, his need for friends was demonstrated in a most convincing manner. At the Last Supper Jesus spoke of his friendship with his chosen twelve. At that critical time they were not just anointed, called, and chosen ministers or authorities as much as they were friends. This meant the most to him. "Greater love hath no man than this, that a man lay down his life for his friends. Ye are my friends. . . . Henceforth I call you not servants . . . but I have called you friends" (John 15:13–15). It was for his friends that Christ would die. His love for them and their love for him provided much of the needed courage to face the suffering that awaited him. Are we not included in that friendship?

Arriving at Gethsemane, Jesus asked three of these friends to share in a deeper way the trial that awaited him. How very human it is that the Son of God, who so frequently called himself the Son of man, would need the cushioning, surrounding love of friends when facing his most difficult hour. "And he took with him Peter and the two sons of Zebedee, and began to be sorrowful and very heavy. Then saith he unto them, My soul is exceeding sorrowful, even unto death: tarry ye here, and watch with me" (Matthew 26:37-38).

If it was needful for the atoning Christ himself to have nearby friends to watch with him, how much more is it needful for us? How much more should we offer our friendship to each other? He had told the disciples earlier, at the Last Supper, "I am not alone, because the Father is with me" (John 16:32). Yet he still desired the supporting company of a human voice, a human touch, and human eyes watching, waiting, upholding by their very presence and thus helping him in his heavy hour.

There follows in Matthew's account the poignant prayer so beloved by Christians of all faiths as Jesus bows to the will of the Father. After having offered it, though, he desired human contact, the reassuring presence of friends, and he arose from prayer to find them. "And he cometh unto the disciples, and findeth them asleep" (Matthew 26:40). After a gentle rebuke to Peter, followed by the assurance that he knew Peter's heart was willing even though his flesh was heavy with sleep, Jesus returned to commune with his Father. The touching prayer of submission was offered again, and we can suppose that with it came the answer he undoubtedly knew the Father would give before the words were spoken. "O my Father, if this cup may not pass away from me, except I drink it, thy will be done" (Matthew 26:42). What he was suffering and what still awaited him pressed down upon him, and once again he sought the solace of human association. He returned to his friends. "And he came and found them asleep again: for their eyes were heavy" (Matthew 26:43). There is a beauty beyond expression in these moments, but we sense it as we read and visualize the events of

Gethsemane. The Savior's need for human support and human friendship was acute, even though he was one with the Father.

I find it significant that even at the moment of betrayal, Jesus addressed Judas with, "Friend, wherefore art thou come?" (Matthew 26:50). If Judas was called friend, what must those of us who love and honor Christ be?

When the shadow of our own cross darkens the sky, when we bend to the Father, beseeching, "Abba, Father, all things are possible unto thee; take away this cup from me" (Mark 14:36), we have the examples of the Savior and of Joseph Smith to guide us. Let us seek out our friends or let us be those friends watching nearby. In our adversities we can and will turn outward; we will await the promised good we know God will bring; we will find assurance in the knowledge that our trials will end and the tears will be wiped away; we will follow Elijah, Moses, and Joshua and move to action; and we will rely on the bounty and love of friends. Thus we will endure well all that life brings to us.

—⚡︎—

CHAPTER FIVE

I was not in safety, neither had I rest,
neither was I quiet; yet trouble came.

Job 3:26

Thou Art Not Yet as Job

The Difficult Question

What do we do when there are no friends to whom we can go for understanding or when those friends we do have fail us? The Lord told Joseph Smith in Liberty Jail, "Thou art not yet as Job; thy friends do not contend against thee" (D&C 121:10). There may be times of adversity that we face, as did Job, essentially alone. Because the story of Job is the quintessential story of suffering, let us examine it more closely.

The story of Job is contained in that part of the Old Testament called the wisdom literature. Job and such books as Ecclesiastes strive to examine some of the deepest and most difficult questions of life. In the case of Job we delve into the problem of suffering—why is it allowed, especially to the righteous? Great scriptural personalities have also asked the corollary to this question—why do the wicked seem to prosper? Perhaps even more important, Job examines a question we all must face at some time in our lives: If everything we hold dear were taken away from us and we were plunged into deep trials, would we still hold to our faith? Would we still love, trust, and honor our Father in Heaven? That is a difficult question to answer, short of experiencing Job-like adversity, which none of us would wish for.

Job is introduced to us as a man that is "perfect and upright, and one that feared God, and eschewed evil" (Job 1:1). We will soon see just how righteous he is! The writer of Job gives his book a framework consisting of two conversations between God and Satan and then a series of debates between Job and his friends. They, we discover, are not really friends—they are not helpful in the least. The book then concludes with an answer from God.

Most of the book of Job is devoted to the conversations between Job and his friends. In his friends' reasoning, God cannot be unjust. Suffering must have a cause, and sin must be that cause. Therefore, in their simplistic understanding of life, Job has sinned. An alternate explanation—that for no apparent reason God would allow the pain endured by Job—challenged their idea of God's justice, which conclusion Job's friends cannot admit. The problem must be in Job. Their answer is shallow and helps us not at all, but their thinking is still dominant throughout the world. Even in our own contemplations of life's experiences, we may equate negative life experiences with lack of worthiness when in reality the truth is far more complicated. Job categorically rejects his friends' answer, and his tenacious holding onto his integrity holds the question constantly before us: Why?

The Lord, who is proud of Job and confident in him, tells Satan, "There is none like him in the earth, a perfect and an upright man" (Job 1:8). It might be helpful here to mention something about the nature of scriptural stories. They tend to be extreme examples. Sarah's waiting decades for the birth of Isaac, for example, is an extreme story of patiently waiting for God to fulfill his promises. Abraham's then being willing to offer Isaac on the top of Mount Moriah reaches the epitome of God asking of his child the supreme sacrifice. Moroni's living alone without friends or family is a quintessential story of loneliness. By their acute nature such stories can embrace all lesser examples and offer counsel to everyone.

Few will suffer as Job did, but few are as devoted and obedient as Job was. Job represents the very righteous, almost perfect individual. If any deserve to avoid suffering, would not it be such a one? He must also receive suffering in an extreme degree, far beyond what most experience on earth. His example then becomes deeply instructive and relevant to all. Job represents humanity—all of humanity, specifically suffering humanity.

"Naked Shall I Return"

Satan is called "the accuser of our brethren" in Revelation. He accuses man "before our God day and night" (Revelation 12:10). In Job we get an idea of this role of the adversary. In response to God's assertion of the goodness of Job, Satan replies, "Doth Job fear God for nought? Hast not thou made an hedge about him, and about his house, and about all that he hath on every side? thou hast blessed the work of his hands, and his substance is increased in the land. But put forth thine hand now, and touch all that he hath, and he will curse thee to thy face" (Job 1:9–11).

This is a serious challenge, and one Satan would level at us all. Do I serve God because he has been so good to me? Many of us have been blessed in unparalleled ways considering the manner in which most people have lived since the dawn of creation. What if all we have was lost in a short period of time? This would be adversity at its nightmare level. That is what happens to Job.

God, still confident in his servant, replies, "All that he hath is in thy power; only upon himself put not forth thine hand" (Job 1:12). Wouldn't it be wonderful to know that God had such assurance in our own faith? There follows a brief account of the beginning of Job's trials as all that he has is destroyed. He is temporally and financially broken. One might at this moment think, "At least I have my family. We can build again." But word soon comes that a storm from the wilderness has blown down the house his children were gathered in, and none of them survived. It is at this news that Job "arose, and rent his mantle, and shaved his head, and fell down on the ground, and worshipped, and said, Naked I came out of my mother's womb, and naked shall I return thither: the Lord gave, and the Lord hath taken away; blessed be the name of the Lord" (Job 1:20-21).

Job has triumphed over Satan's accusation. He can still trust and love God in his extremity. We are specifically told Job "sinned not, nor charged God foolishly" (Job 1:22). In such situations it is tempting to wonder who is running the world. We may counsel God, complain of his justice, question his love, and turn away, but Job does none of those things. We wonder as we read Job's words how he can respond so positively, but life is going to get worse for Job.

Once again we are brought to the throne of God to listen to the conversation between the Lord of heaven and the lord of hell. God, still confident in his son, tells Satan with pride, "Still he holdeth fast his integrity, although thou movedst me against him, to destroy him without cause" (Job 2:3). Those last words are critical: We must remember Job's suffering is without cause. There are times when we cannot make any sense out of the cruelty and apparent indiscriminate suffering of man. If there were a cause, perhaps, we could understand it, change it, and thereby end the trial.

Satan counters with one more attempt on the integrity of Job. "Skin for skin," he responds, "all that a man hath will he give for his life. But put forth thine hand now, and touch his bone and his flesh, and he will curse thee to thy face" (Job 2:4-5). The loss of external sources of joy and comfort is one thing, but what about physical pain? In their agony, men will turn against God for not preventing it. Did not God, as Satan reminds Jesus on the pinnacle of the temple, promise that he would watch out for us, giving his angels charge over us, even to preventing the stubbing of our toes? (see Matthew 4:5-6). What, then, should we think of severe pain? Job's flesh is covered with boils. He removes himself to the ash heap outside of town, takes a potsherd, and scrapes his skin with it. He is the perfect picture of dejection and misery, a man apparently totally forgotten of God—abandoned without cause.

This is the story that becomes the foundation for an exploration of human suffering. Let us look deeper into the goodness of Job and into the intensity and quality of his agony.

Should any man as true as Job have to endure such horrors? Job's friends do come and sit silently with him in his mourning. So far, so good. They sense his confusion and his dominant question, which becomes theirs: Why? Why has this happened? Would there not be some comfort in knowing the causes and consequences of it all? In Job's friends' limited and ungracious perspective, the only reason they can see is that Job has offended God. In other words, Job somehow deserves what has happened. The solution is therefore simple. He must find which sin he has committed, repent, and trust in the forgiving mercy of a generous and pardoning God. The only problem is that Job cannot find any action sufficient to explain his misery, though he searches his memory and his life thoroughly. In his replies to the friends, we learn of his goodness and of additional aspects of his wretchedness.

"I Will Not Remove Mine Integrity"

The integrity of Job is vast indeed. Eliphaz, one of his friends, says to him, "Thou hast strengthened the weak hands. Thy words have upholden him that was falling, and thou hast strengthened the feeble knees" (Job 4:3-4). Job has apparently been the type of friend we would all like to have to see us through our trials. Later Job tells his "miserable comforters": "If your soul were in my soul's stead . . . I would strengthen you with my mouth, and the moving of my lips should asswage your grief" (Job 16:2, 4-5).

Concerning the commandments, Job tells us, "My foot hath held his steps, his way have I kept, and not declined" (Job 23:11). He has been generous and charitable to the poor. "I delivered the poor that cried, and the fatherless, and him that had none to help him. . . . I caused the widow's heart to sing for joy. . . . I was eyes to the blind, and feet was I to the lame. I was a father to the poor: and the cause which I knew not I searched out" (Job 29:12-13, 15-16).

Even inwardly, in his thoughts and emotions, Job was righteous. "I made a covenant with mine eyes; why then should I think upon a maid? . . . If I have made gold my hope, or have said to the fine gold, Thou art my confidence. . . . If I rejoiced at the destruction of him that hated me . . . neither have I suffered my mouth to sin by wishing a curse to his soul. . . . If my land cry against me, or that the furrows likewise thereof complain; . . . The words of Job are ended" (Job 31:1, 24, 29-30, 38, 40).

These are but a small sampling of the areas of his life Job

examines to see if the accusation of his friends is worthy of consideration. Yet as he delves into the minutest corners of his thoughts and behavior, he can find nothing worthy of such a high degree of pain. Besides, he tells his friends, if I have sinned, should not a gracious God forgive me instead of destroying me, because my heart is so full of love for him? "Why dost thou not pardon my transgression," he calls out to God, "and take away mine iniquity? . . . Shew me wherefore thou contendest with me. . . . Thou knowest that I am not wicked" (Job 7:21; 10:2, 7).

I wonder how many of us could defend ourselves to the degree Job does. He is without question a "perfect and an upright man, one that feareth God, and escheweth evil" (Job 1:8). His story meets the criteria of the type of stories that the scriptures provide. Now let us discuss the additions to his suffering.

"Oh That My Grief Were Thoroughly Weighed"

If we visualize a balance, which the book of Job invites us to do, what can we lay on the suffering side of the scale? We already know he has lost all his possessions and his family. We know his wife is no comfort or solace to him. Her words echo the adversary's own, urging him to do exactly what Satan anticipates he will do. "Dost thou still retain thine integrity? curse God, and die" (Job 2:9). Later Job tells us, "My breath is strange to my wife, though I entreated for the children's sake of mine own body" (Job 19:17). Can he expect help or comfort from any other source? We know his friends have failed him, and so has everybody else. "My brethren [are] far from me, and mine acquaintance are verily estranged from me. My kinsfolk have failed, and my familiar friends have forgotten me. . . . I am an alien in their sight. I called my servant, and he gave me no answer. . . . They whom I loved are turned against me" (Job 19:13-16, 19).

There is a tendency for the fallen natural man to rejoice over the fall of a once-respected and worthy man. In our day, the tabloids and newscasts provide ample proof of this quality of man. Job becomes the butt of jokes and the subject of derisive songs. The man once sought out for his wisdom is out of favor. "Unto me men gave ear, and waited, and kept silence at my counsel" (Job 29:21); "But now they that are younger than I have me in derision. . . . And now am I their song, yea, I am their byword. They abhor me, they flee far from me, and spare not to spit in my face. . . . Upon my right hand rise the youth; they push away my feet" (Job 30:1, 9-10, 12); "Yea, young children despised me; I arose, and they spake against me" (Job 19:18). Laughed at, mocked, tripped by young children, the once respected Job is safer on his ash heap outside of his village.

When we are in deep pain, we may find release in the peace and forgetfulness of sleep. But even this quietus is denied Job. "When I lie down, I say, When shall I arise, and the night be gone? and I am full of tossings to and fro unto the dawning of the day. . . . When I say, My bed shall comfort me, my couch shall ease my complaint; then thou scarest me with dreams, and terrifiest me through visions" (Job 7:4, 13-14). For Job, sleep is fleeting, and when it does come, it brings nightmares.

Even the expectation of better days, of an end to his agony, is denied Job. "My days are swifter than a weaver's shuttle, and are spent without hope. . . . Mine eye shall no more see good" (Job 7:6-7). The last hope for the hopeless is death, the one power over Job that God would not allow Satan. The irony of this is unmistakable, for death would be a release, and Job longs for it. "Wherefore is light given to him that is in misery, and life unto the bitter in soul; which long for death, but it cometh not" (Job 3:20–21).

We could examine other verses, but these are sufficient to see the boundaries of Job's life. He even has the added pain of remembering the better days. It would be one thing to be born into a life of poverty and rejection, hopelessness and despair, but to experience the contrast that Job does is quite another. Considering the goodness we have seen Job enjoying and the suffering he is enduring, it is no wonder that Job says, "I am full of confusion" (Job 10:15). That confusion and the perplexing contrast between his former and present life are but an additional element in the suffering and pain he is trying to endure without accusing God of injustice.

"What Is Man?"

What are we to do with such a story as that of Job? We can close our eyes to human suffering and pretend that such extremities do not exist, but to a degree there are Jobs all over the world, and the relevance of his story to our lives cannot be ignored. Job asks a question that restored truths help us begin to answer in order to make some sense out of the suffering of life.

"Am I a sea, or a whale, that thou settest a watch over me? . . . What is man, that thou shouldest magnify him? and that thou shouldest set thine heart upon him? And that thou shouldest visit him every morning, and try him every moment?" (Job 7:12, 17–18). In Job's mind he is insignificant. He is not so grand or important that God should be involved in his life. To what purpose, then, is all he is passing through?

God revealed to Moses that his work and glory was to bring to pass the immortality and eternal life of man. It is God's design to make us all gods, to live life qualitatively like his own. If we were to ask ourselves, What is God like? our answers would include such attributes as kindness, longsuffering, patience, meekness, compassion, mercy. At times, pushed to the extreme by life's adversities, we may be tempted to think that God is also indifferent, but this we must not do.

As we have learned from Paul, the experiences of life that best instill perfection in the human soul are what we might call the negative ones. In order to magnify man, it seems as if God must put him through the fire of suffering. I have often wondered what I would do if I could change the world. As a father, what if I knew that the example of my own suffering would create in the hearts, souls, and minds of my children the very perfection of God? Would I choose to end those sufferings? I think not. I believe—of course it is easy, absent any real adversity, to say—that I would be willing to suffer any pain if I knew that my pain was producing in my children those wonderful, godly characteristics of mercy, longsuffering, compassion, and kindness. Would I allow my children to endure adversities of a despairing kind if I knew one child's distress was creating godliness in her brothers and sisters? I am not sure I can answer that. It is easy to answer yes from the comfort of my office with my fingers on the keyboard, but in the moment when a loved child is crying out in pain, would I not end that child's suffering? Perhaps God must "visit [us] every morning, and try [us] every moment" to shape us into the eternal creatures we are destined to become. Is the pain worth the outcome?

That is a difficult question and one we will try to answer later, especially as it relates to the suffering of children. If God has all wisdom and all love, the afflictions of mortality must be necessary and, as Paul assured us, the final outcome must be worthy of the sufferings, even Job-like suffering. Expounding the theory is easy, but experientially our hearts and minds search for justice that we have attributed to a personal and loving God—our Father.

Our task is to pass through the proving ground of mortality as well as Job did. To live a life as he lived it, then at least we can avoid the deeper pains of guilt. If we were given the choice of suffering without cause, as Job suffered, or suffering as David did after the murder of Uriah, surely we would all choose Job's path. The pangs of a distressed conscience may be the greatest known to man. Perhaps that is why we go to such lengths to rationalize, blame, justify, or deny conscience. Nonetheless, the pangs of conscience are pains we have some control over because of our agency. Job endured in part because he knew that he was a good man, despite the biting words of his three friends. There is a measure of comfort in being able to say, as did Job, "When he hath tried me, I shall come forth as gold" and "Till I die I will not remove mine integrity from me" (Job 23:10; 27:5).

We can also maintain our faith, for we know so little, as God soon demonstrates to Job. Job's trust and confidence in God are perhaps the most exemplary in all of scripture, for he says, "Though he slay me, yet will I trust in him. . . . He also shall be my salvation" (Job 13:15–16). And, as did Job, our task is to silence the accusation of Satan. We can trust and love God in spite of what the world brings. We will not curse God and die. Though we may be in total confusion, we can say as did Job, "I know that my redeemer liveth" (Job 19:25). When we know that our Redeemer lives, we know what is sufficient to survive life in the midst of confusion and adversity, just as Job endured in the bewilderment of his own terrible situation.

God's Reply

The writer of the book of Job records the Lord speaking to Job and his accusing friends in the last chapters. It is a somewhat anticlimactic ending to the powerful themes of Job, but some closure must be offered. The power of the book of Job is in the dilemma and the moving speeches of its protagonist. The questions it asks cause us to look inward to see if we would refute Satan's charge, and they give the book of Job all the justification it needs to hold a place in the holy canon. But God does speak.

Starting in chapter 38, the Lord asks Job a series of questions concerning the creation: "Where wast thou when I laid the foundations of the earth? declare, if thou hast understanding" (Job 38:4). The questions continue throughout four chapters and cover everything from the weather to the flight of birds. Of course Job—and even we in our modern, scientifically literate world—cannot answer the questions. We are infants standing on the vast shore of knowledge. Do we even have the capacity to understand the simplest of things, let alone what God is doing with men? We must simply trust. Job concludes, "I know that thou canst do every thing, and that no thought can be withholden from thee. . . . I uttered that I understood not; things too wonderful for me, which I knew not" (Job 42:2–3).

The questions God asks Job are not simply to show God's superior knowledge but to create in Job and in us a sense of wonder at the sheer majesty of his creation. Surely a God who creates such wonders as a habitation for his children, wonders which are beyond our capacity to appreciate, is a God worthy of trust. Such a God would take particular care of his own child and be attentive to the needs of that child, even at the price of pain. When the Psalmist faced similar questions, God answered, "Be still, and know that I am God" (Psalm 46:10). God does not reason with Job by telling him why God has allowed such affliction; rather, he appeals to Job's (and our) heart, a heart which, like that of a child, trusts his Father. That trust is not unfounded in light of the majesty and beauty we see around us.

"Like Hinds' Feet"

The little-known experiences of Habakkuk center on themes similar to those experienced by Job, but Habakkuk ends with such a lovely image it might be helpful to include it. Habakkuk questioned, as others have, the manner in which God was governing the world. Sometimes it may seem that God is unaware or is indifferent to our plight; otherwise, why would he leave matters as they are? In words that remind us both of the Prophet Joseph and of Job, Habakkuk cries out, "O Lord, how long shall I cry, and thou wilt not hear! even cry out unto thee of violence, and thou wilt not save! Why dost thou . . . cause me to behold grievance? . . . Judgment doth never go forth" (Habakkuk 1:2–4). Habakkuk is distressed by a world where nothing makes sense, where "the law is slacked," where "the wicked doth compass about the righteous" (Habakkuk 1:4).

What distresses him most is the injustice of it all. Is not God a God of justice? How then can he allow such suffering, especially the suffering of the innocent at the hands of the cruel? We shall fully examine this theme in a future chapter. "Thou art of purer eyes than to behold evil, and canst not look on iniquity: wherefore lookest thou upon them that deal treacherously, and holdest thy tongue when the wicked devoureth the man that is more righteous than he? And makest men as the fishes of the sea, as the creeping things, that have no ruler over them?" (Habakkuk 1:13–14). The last sentence of that scripture refers to the law of the jungle. Surely men should not live in a world where the strong and the mighty can with impunity victimize and dominate the weak. But we see that Habakkuk has observed the world correctly in many instances. His questions are not far from the thoughts most of us have entertained and will probably wrestle with throughout our lives.

Among the words that God gives Habakkuk as an answer is a phrase that Paul, in particular, echoed in his writings: "The just shall live by his faith" (Habakkuk 2:4; see also Romans 1:17). "The vision is yet for an appointed time, but at the end it shall speak, and not lie: though it tarry, wait for it; because it will surely come, it will not tarry" (Habakkuk 2:3). The Lord seems to be saying, Give me time. From your perspective, it may seem as if no one is in control, but in time you will see. In the meantime, you must have faith and trust me.

That is essentially the answer given to Job.

Habakkuk accepts the Lord's answer. His trust is founded in faith, and yet he knows how fragile that faith can be when an individual is faced with the sometimes absurd cruelties and sufferings of life. He ends with a prayer of assuring faith and requested help:

"Although the fig tree shall not blossom, neither shall fruit be in the vines; the labour of the olive shall fail, and the fields shall yield no meat; the flock shall be cut off from the fold, and there shall be no herd in the stalls: Yet I will rejoice in the Lord, I will joy in the God of my salvation" (Habakkuk 3:17–18).

This is Habakkuk's espousal of trust. To paraphrase, he says: No matter how broken I am; no matter if everything is taken away, as in the case of Job, I will not only trust but rejoice in God. As he counseled me, I will wait. But hold me to my faith and my trust. Let me not slip.

Notice the beautiful image with which Habakkuk concludes: "The Lord God is my strength, and he will make my feet like hinds' feet, and he will make me to walk upon mine high places" (Habakkuk 3:19).

On backpacking trips to Glacier National Park, I marveled at the mountain goats that could walk along the narrowest of cliffs. In Israel, along the cliffs bordering the Dead Sea, I have seen ibex walking along ledges barely an inch wide. Any moment, I have thought, they will tumble to their deaths. Yet their tiny but sturdy hooves cling to those tiny holds. In a similar way our faith is often tested; we may feel we are holding onto our trust in God by the most infinitely small margins. It may feel to us that with one false step, we will fall from our high place, our world of faith and confidence in God. Like Habakkuk, we must rely on our Father in Heaven that he will make our feet as hinds' feet so that we may never fall off the narrow path that we are instructed to walk, a path that adversity and pain often narrow to the tiniest limits.

"Return, and Discern"

Though not as intense in its questioning of God's wisdom in allowing suffering and the apparent injustice of righteous people suffering while wicked people prosper, the book of Malachi poses similar questions. "Your words have been stout against me, saith the Lord. Yet ye say, What have we spoken so much against thee?" (Malachi 3:13). Though the people have not openly challenged the Lord as Habakkuk or Job did, their musing and questioning have not gone unnoticed.

Habakkuk said, "I will stand upon my watch, and set me upon the tower, and will watch to see what he will say unto me" (Habakkuk 2:1). He was not afraid to bring up the issue with God. The people in the book of Malachi, though wondering, hesitate to confront the Lord, so he brings up the issue himself: "Ye have said, It is vain to serve God: and what profit is it that we have kept his ordinance, and that we have walked mournfully before the Lord of

Hosts? And now we call the proud happy; yea, they that work wickedness are set up; yea, they that tempt God are even delivered" (Malachi 3:14-15).

What kind of world is this? Why be righteous? It does not seem to matter in the least. The wicked are not suffering any negative consequences; quite the contrary—all is well with them. Job also marked this observation when he told his critical friends, "The tabernacles of robbers prosper, and they that provoke God are secure" (Job 12:6).

Life does seem to present such a picture from time to time. Perhaps God wanted us to be good for the sake of goodness. If righteousness was always immediately rewarded and wickedness quickly punished, self-interest would make us godly and fear would compel us to sainthood. Because it is often otherwise, however, our commitment to goodness, integrity, and decency must be inspired by deeper resources than mere outward and immediate consequences.

God does answer the confused people of Malachi's time. They—and we, with them—are told God keeps a "book of remembrance" containing the names of those who reverence him (see Malachi 3:16). God will remember and bless those who lived a virtuous life, even in a world that does not seem to care for the virtuous or respond to them. Those who refuse evil will be remembered and rewarded, even in a world where, it appears, evil pays: "They shall be mine, saith the Lord of hosts, in that day when I make up my jewels; . . . Then shall ye return, and discern between the righteous and the wicked, between him that serveth God and him that serveth him not" (Malachi 3:17-18).

We have to be patient and wait. This answer was less satisfactory to me when I was younger, but as I have grown older and seen more of life, I have come to trust the Lord's answer.

I recall being quite envious as a young man of some of my friends who were not raised in the stricter environment of the gospel. Though when I was young I thought my mother was strict, she gave her children a great deal of autonomy. I would not have participated in some of the questionable activities of some of my friends, even if the opportunity presented itself, but I often thought that no great negative consequences were flowing to my friends from their actions and no great blessings were flowing to me as a result of keeping the standards. Fifteen- and sixteen-year-olds do not often possess long-term wisdom; I certainly didn't. Decades later, I can see the difference between their lives and my own. I would not trade places with them for anything in the world. I can now return and discern, seeing how different their lives are from mine, and I am grateful that my mother taught me to trust in God's goodness and wisdom.

The Complex Arithmetic

From a philosophic point of view, trust in God may not be completely satisfactory, but the books of Job, Habakkuk, and Malachi tackle difficult questions. Other books of scripture that tackle such questions include Jeremiah. Perhaps the answers these books offer can be considered at best incomplete, because we cannot see a sufficient reason for such events as the Holocaust, the Stalinist purges, the Cambodian killing fields, or any of the other genocides still perpetrated around the world. We are compelled by the justice ingrained in our souls to wonder at the reason God allows these events. No truly thinking individual with love for his or her fellowman can help but wonder and ask the Lord, sometimes quite pointedly, as did past prophets.

Elie Wiesel, a Nobel laureate, a distinguished author, and a

Holocaust survivor, wrote a play called *The Trial of God,* based on an experience he claimed to have witnessed as a prisoner in Auschwitz in which a few of his fellow prisoners put God on trial for allowing what was happening to them. When asked recently if the story from Auschwitz was real, he replied in the affirmative; however, he placed the setting of his play in the Russian pogroms of the 1600s. Whether the story that inspired his play is true or not, the play Wiesel wrote addresses a serious dilemma: What evidence was there of God's love for the Jewish people and of his keeping his covenant with them? Can a people who have suffered the horrific ordeals of Nazi Germany, let alone centuries of pogroms and purges of Europe, continue to believe in the God of the Bible—in the God of the Psalms? If God is omnipotent, he could stop such evils. If he is unable to stop them, how do we continue to believe in him? If he can stop them and does not, his morality is less than ours. If he chooses not to stop such things but has good reasons for such a choice, no one has yet adequately proposed those reasons. Where do we go from here? The mock court decided against God. They could find no excuse or circumstance that would justify his apparent indifference. So what should one do now? Let us go and pray was their answer.[1] What other answer are we left with?

Prophets, authors of great literature, and philosophers have all tackled the problem of suffering. If anyone had given the definitive answer, we would not still be struggling to measure life's meaning against the scale of pain and crippling adversity. And, I suppose, the books of Job, Habakkuk, and Malachi provide stories of suffering to which many can relate and to which God can refer when comforting those who, like Joseph Smith—and us—need his solace when facing a trial like that of Liberty Jail.

To find sufficient wisdom and strength to endure and to

endure well may be all we are offered by the scriptures or an omniscient God. We may not be capable of understanding the complex arithmetic of a God who lives in infinity, who creates galaxies. We may find ourselves echoing Jeremiah's words: "Righteous art thou, O Lord, when I plead with thee: yet let me talk with thee of thy judgments" (Jeremiah 12:1). We may find ourselves praying, "I know thou art good and loving, Father, but what about . . . ?" Where does that leave us—with Elie Wiesel's jury? We will go and pray; we will echo Nephi, who told the angel, "I know that [God] loveth his children; nevertheless, I do not know the meaning of all things" (1 Nephi 11:17). And we will continue to search his holy scriptures for the clarification, comfort, and insight he offers so that the "meaning of all things" may become less opaque.

—⚉—

CHAPTER SIX

In all their affliction he was afflicted,
and the angel of his presence saved them: in his love
and in his pity he redeemed them; and he bare
them, and carried them all the days of old.

Isaiah 63:9

TEARS UPON THE MOUNTAINS

"Of More Importance Than They All"

We are missing one thing in the book of Job that is critical to understanding adversity. We do not see God close up. He remains somewhat distant, even perhaps a little aloof. The author of the book of Job leaves us hungering for the tone of voice, facial expressions, or touch of a Heavenly Father rather than a grand examiner presenting question after question before a humble and ignorant student. We long for the face-to-face encounter of other scriptural accounts, an expression that suggests the relationship of friends. This touch of personality, this quality of character, is essential if we are to recognize it and receive it when our own houses figuratively come crashing down upon us, as the house actually did upon Job's children. That we may know the music of God's soul as he watches over, presides over, allows, creates—whatever word or phrase one might favor—the adversities of our lives, the Lord has filled the scriptures with stories to reveal the inner reality of who he is and how he feels.

Perhaps a good place to begin is with Alma's great sermon to the Saints who lived in the valley of Gideon. Though there are many wonderful prophecies, Alma testifies "there is one thing which is of more importance than they all—for behold, the time is not far distant that the Redeemer liveth and cometh among his people" (Alma 7:7). Christ, the Creator of worlds, the Son of the Eternal Father, is going to live among men and experience life as they do. The more distant and powerful God of Heaven becomes the very near and personal Only Begotten Son. He came to live in the poorest of circumstances, and he left it after suffering an ignominious death.

Notice in the following verses from Alma's address the specific types of mortal experiences the Savior came to understand at the human level. "And he shall go forth, suffering *pains* and *afflictions* and *temptations* of every kind; and this that the word might be fulfilled which saith he will take upon him the pains and the *sicknesses* of his people. And he will take upon him *death* . . . and he will take upon him their *infirmities*, that his bowels may be filled with mercy, according to the flesh, that he may know according to the flesh how to succor his people according to their infirmities" (Alma 7:11–12; emphasis added).

Alma presents a profound portrayal of the Son of God. Six words in his account dominate the life experience of Jesus Christ—*pains, afflictions, temptations, sicknesses, death, infirmities*. These would be "of every kind." These he wished to know "according to the flesh," meaning to experience them at our level. This is to know life on the side of suffering. Isaiah taught that Jesus would be "a man of sorrows, and acquainted with grief" (Isaiah 53:3). Jesus also knew love, joy, laughter, friendship, family, and all the positive things life offers. Since, according to Lehi, righteousness and happiness are synonymous, Jesus certainly was the happiest man who lived, but in order to succor us—to run to help us—he had to taste life's bitter side too.

Paul taught these same truths in his Epistle to the Hebrews: "For verily he took not on him the nature of angels; but he took on him the seed of Abraham. Wherefore in all things it behoved him to be made like unto his brethren, that he might be . . . merciful and faithful. . . . For in that he himself hath suffered being tempted, he is able to succour them that are tempted" (Hebrews 2:16–18). *Tempted* in this context means not only to entice to sin but also, and more generally, to face the trials of life.

When we converse with individuals who are undergoing adversity, we often say "I understand." This we say sincerely, but sometimes we see in their eyes a questioning look that seems to reply, "Do you really? How can you when you have not gone through the same thing?" We can understand to a point by applying sympathy, a wonderful gift that is enhanced by the Holy Spirit. We try to put ourselves in their place and it works—to a degree. Other times we have been through similar trials, and we "mourn with those who mourn . . . and comfort those that stand in need of comfort" (Mosiah 18:9). We have true empathy because we have been through the same experiences. Then when we say "I understand" there is a greater power behind it. Of the two ways of saying "I understand," one in which we imagine ourselves in the place of the sufferer, and one in which we have experienced the same kind of suffering, which did Christ wish to be able to say to us? Alma tells us, "Now the Spirit knoweth all things; nevertheless the Son of God suffereth according to the flesh" (Alma 7:13). Through the power of the Spirit,

Jesus could have comprehended our sorrows, but he wanted to know them from our perspective that he might not only be merciful but "filled with mercy" (Alma 7:12).

We have the assurance that our Savior not only knows our griefs and pains, not only understands them but feels them from a mortal perspective, the mortality he inherited from his mother, Mary. This he demonstrated numerous times in the scriptures. Let us examine a few.

"I Have Surely Seen . . ."

One of the central stories of scripture is that of the Exodus. Its themes are referred to numerous times throughout the full canon. Individuals from Alma to Jesus referred to it and made its details relevant to their own times and circumstances. The story begins in adversity and affliction.

The Egyptians, who throughout scriptural history became synonymous with oppression, "did set over [the children of Israel] taskmasters to afflict them with their burdens. . . . But the more they afflicted them, the more they multiplied" (Exodus 1:11-12). Almost immediately we are given a great truth in this story. Even in the midst of overwhelming burdens and affliction a person—or in this case, a people—can still thrive.

We are taught this same truth in Jacob's quoting of the allegory of the tame and wild olive trees. If we read this allegory as a parable, new possibilities for application are called forth. The various branches scattered in different parts of the vineyard represent the people of the world. Remember that some were planted in poor soil, poor enough that the servant questioned the wisdom of his master in planting them there.

Perhaps you have questioned your own planting in the mortal

vineyard of the world. But we are assured that the Lord had nourished the branches "this long time" (Jacob 5:20). "Counsel me not," he later said. "I knew that it was a poor spot of ground; wherefore, I said unto thee, I have nourished it this long time, and thou beholdest that it hath brought forth much fruit." The Lord then pointed out a branch in even poorer soil, which due to his nurturing had "brought forth much fruit" (Jacob 5:22-23). It seems that a universal truth teaches us that we thrive in adversity, yet often flounder or dwindle in abundance. Even in the most debilitating of circumstances if we respond to the Lord's nourishing we can bring forth wonderful fruits—the fruits of character and godliness, of compassion, empathy, courage and patience. So it is no surprise that the children of Israel could also thrive in spite of their taskmasters.

Because the children of Israel continued to prosper, the Egyptians increased their labors. "And the Egyptians made the children of Israel to serve with rigour: And they made their lives bitter with hard bondage, in morter, and in brick . . . all their service, wherein they made them serve, was with rigour" (Exodus 1:13-14). Most of us know that life can be a mortar and brick existence—a lot of rigorous labor without much to show for it. During these times it is spiritually renewing and necessary to remind ourselves of the Lord's words to Moses from the burning bush. What was true thousands of years ago is true today: "I have surely seen the affliction of my people which are in Egypt, and have heard their cry by reason of their taskmasters; for I know their sorrows; and I am come down to deliver them" (Exodus 3:7-8).

The Lord's deliverance was to send Moses, an Israelite himself. This is the Lord's way! He most often delivers us from adversity through the agency and sympathy of others, including friends, whose role we have already discussed. It is instructive, however, to understand how incapable Moses considered himself concerning his ability to soften and remove the adversity of his people. "Who am I," he asks the Lord, "that I should bring forth the children of Israel out of Egypt?" (Exodus 3:11).

We may feel a similar inadequacy when we become the Lord's agents for removing or comforting the sorrows of one we love. Moses was assured, however—and we may likewise be assured—that "certainly I will be with thee" (Exodus 3:12).

There is a type or foreshadowing in the Lord's words from the burning bush, for in time he would actually come to experience the sorrows of mankind and deliver us, to "be with" us. Let us examine a few examples of his ministry by way of illustration.

"Jesus Wept"

The shortest verse in all scripture contains two simple words— "Jesus wept" (John 11:35). To know the context of that verse is to see into the heart of God. The occasion is the raising of Lazarus from the dead. Jesus has retired to the east side of the Jordan River to find a measure of peace and protection from the hostility and danger he encountered in Judea and Jerusalem. Mary and Martha live in Bethany, on the east side of the Mount of Olives just a short walk from Jerusalem. When he receives word from the sisters that Lazarus is sick, Jesus waits two days before crossing the river and ascending the hills to Bethany. His disciples warn him about returning to Judea, but he knew before his departure exactly what he would do upon arriving in Bethany. He will raise Lazarus from the dead. It is very important that we know this for the full beauty of his weeping to be realized. He decided to raise Lazarus before he sees either Martha or Mary.

Both sisters greet Jesus with the words, "Lord, if thou hadst been here, my brother had not died." Jesus now surveys the scene around him. Mary is at his feet weeping, and others have come with her. "When Jesus therefore saw her weeping, and the Jews also weeping which came with her, he *groaned in the spirit,* and was *troubled,* and said, Where have ye laid him? They said unto him, Lord, come and see. Jesus wept" (John 11:32–35; emphasis added).

Remember, Jesus knows what he is going to do! He knows that within a few minutes all the tears and sorrow will be turned to joy with the return of Lazarus from the grave. Yet, he still weeps, and his weeping is not a surface flow of tears—it is a groaning, troubled, expression of sharing their grief. He feels their sorrow as if it were his own. He feels it, knowing it will only last a few more moments, but the intensity of his empathy cannot be doubted. Thus bearing their burden as if it were his own, he turns toward the grave. "Jesus therefore again *groaning in himself* cometh to the grave" (John 11:38; emphasis added). His understanding, his feeling their pain, continues to the very moment their sorrow turns to joy when he utters the words, "Lazarus, come forth" (John 11:43).

We recognize a similar moment of unity with humanity during Christ's visit to the Nephites and Lamanites as recorded in 3 Nephi. Sensitive to the people's desire that he remain with them a little longer, Jesus called their little children to him. When they had gathered around him and knelt on the ground, "Jesus groaned within himself, and said: Father, I am troubled because of the wickedness of the people of the house of Israel" (3 Nephi 17:14). This groaning, similar to that shared with Mary and Martha, is more general, whereas theirs was specific. These children will live during the most peaceful and happy period of Book of Mormon history. Perhaps he was groaning not just for what they and their parents, as righteous believers in a wicked society, had suffered but for all the children who must suffer in the world due to the wickedness of men, for all those who would not live a life of love as would those who knelt at his feet. Jesus then knelt with the little children. We are told that the prayer he uttered was so deeply beautiful that it filled the hearts of all who heard it with joy and that it could not be recorded. Yet even then, after such beauty and impassioned prayer, "he took their little children, one by one, and blessed them, and prayed unto the Father for them" (3 Nephi 17:21).

"Woman, Why Weepest Thou?"

There were moments in the Savior's life when he showed a spontaneous compassion that is compelling and wonderful. I have often reflected on the appearance of the resurrected Christ to Mary Magdalene. Was this a planned or a spontaneous demonstration of his ability to feel our sorrows? The choice of the first person to witness the Resurrection may have been decided in the councils of heaven, because it was the turning point of religious history, but there is something about John's account of Christ's appearance at the Garden Tomb that leads me to think this may have been spontaneous.

Mary had been to the tomb early in the morning with the other women. When it was discovered that the body of Jesus was not there, Mary ran to tell Peter and John, who then hurried to the tomb to see for themselves. After their departure, "Mary stood without at the sepulchre weeping: and as she wept, she stooped down, and looked into the sepulchre" (John 20:11). What a natural human reaction! Once again she looks to see that he is really gone. Two angels appear to her and ask, "Woman, why weepest thou? She saith unto them, Because they have taken away my Lord, and I know not where they have laid him" (John 20:13).

But the Savior is nearby. He addresses her, also asking, "Woman, why weepest thou? whom seekest thou?" (John 20:15). Her loving and tender reply must have touched the Savior to his very center. I have never been able to read the following exchange with the tone of quiet love and gentleness I believe it deserves. "Sir, if thou have borne him hence, tell me where thou hast laid him, and I will take him away" (John 20:15). Jesus responds to her poignant words by softly calling her name: "Mary. She turned herself, and saith unto him, Rabboni" (John 20:16). "Whom seekest thou?" We know the answer to that question when it is manifested in our own lives. We seek the Healer.

In the next verse, Joseph Smith changes one word, but that change makes all the difference. "Jesus saith unto her, *Hold* me not; for I am not yet ascended to my Father" (JST John 20:17; emphasis added). Joseph Smith's change, from *touch* to *hold* means, in this context, "Do not detain me." It can also suggest a physical holding, as the other women held his feet when he appeared to them. I cannot imagine a more important report to be made concerning one's ministry and calling than that of Jesus to the Father. He had accomplished the Father's will in all things. The Atonement is finished, the Resurrection begun, the work in the world of spirits initiated.

But a woman is weeping, one who loved and served her Master. I do not believe Jesus could leave Mary without offering the comfort he alone could impart. Her grief touched him deeply, just as Mary's and Martha's sorrow had drawn from him those groaning sighs at the death of Lazarus. "Hold me not," he told her, almost as if she could keep him there if she chose.

Did not the unspoken desires of the multitude at Bountiful

keep the Savior among them a little longer? And in the account of the newly risen Savior, where we are specifically told that the other women had held him by the feet, I think it is safe to assume Mary embraced the Savior or at least fell at his feet as they did. The Savior seems to be saying, "Don't detain me, Mary. I must ascend to my Father; but He is your Father also and your God also." There is a beautiful spontaneity in this encounter that is so revealing of our Savior's compassion and feelings for us. In his own way he comes to us all, asking, "Why weepest thou?"

"How Is It That the Heavens Weep?"

The compassionate nature of the Lord's personality is evident throughout the scriptural record. He wants us to know that he knows, understands, and feels, at the weeping level, our afflictions and sorrows. Should we miss this with Mary and Martha or with Mary Magdalene, we might catch hold of it in another story. One of these is related in the Pearl of Great Price, in the book of Moses. Enoch was shown a vision of future generations. Most of what he saw related to war, bigotry, destruction, and famine—the long, sad litany of human history—depicted so because "the power of Satan was upon all the face of the earth" (Moses 7:24). Enoch also saw the future peace of Zion. Moses uses a well-chosen word to describe all those who are not part of Zion, all those undergoing the turmoil of human disobedience and the pain it causes to both the guilty and the innocent. He calls them "the residue" (Moses 7:20, 22, 28, 43).

At first reading we might think Moses 7 is focused on the people of Zion, but a closer look shows us that the Lord's main concern in this chapter is the residue. How does he respond to their unhappiness, most often brought on by their own foolish choices? Enoch first sees a vision of Satan and his followers laughing and rejoicing over the wickedness of men and the apparent failure of God to keep his children. By contrast—and it is a very powerful contrast—we are shown the face of Deity:

"And it came to pass that the God of heaven looked upon the residue of the people, and he wept; and Enoch bore record of it, saying: How is it that the heavens weep, and shed forth their tears as the rain upon the mountains?" (Moses 7:28). The Lord answers, "Should not the heavens weep, seeing these shall suffer?" (Moses 7:37). If he weeps for the suffering of the residue, for the suffering of those who defy his eternal Fatherhood, how much more so does he weep for the suffering of those striving to be true, as you and I are? God is in the business of ending suffering. The whole plan of salvation is directed to that final outcome; and that is why Alma calls the plan of salvation "the great plan of happiness" (Alma 42:8). As a Church we most often use the phrase "plan of salvation," but it is interchangeable with "plan of happiness." Personally I prefer Alma's phrases "great plan of happiness" or "plan of mercy" (Alma 42:15). Salvation focuses on what Christ will do; happiness, on what we will eventually receive. "Plan of salvation" indicates a process, a series of steps moving one forward on a progressive journey. "Plan of happiness" suggests a state of mind or soul, a condition, not just the result but the state of mind to be enjoyed along the path. Enoch later weeps with the Lord, understanding on a personal level the heart and mind of God. Enoch will not accept the Lord's offered comfort until he knows that sorrow and wickedness will end, mankind will be redeemed, and happiness granted to all.

That moment of discovery is described in beautiful words that are equally true of Christ and his Father, and they encompass each of us in all our adversities: "And it came to pass that the Lord spake unto Enoch, and told Enoch all the doings of the children of men;

wherefore Enoch knew, and looked upon their wickedness, and their misery, and wept and stretched forth his arms, and his heart swelled wide as eternity; and his bowels yearned; and all eternity shook" (Moses 7:41). Eternity overflowed with compassion and empathy. All eternity cannot hold the mercy of God.

"When Thou Walkest through the Fire"

Weeping and groaning in empathy is not sufficient for the Lord; he also walks with us in our dark moments. We lovingly quote David's teaching, "Yea, though I walk through the valley of the shadow of death, I will fear no evil: for thou art with me; thy rod and thy staff they comfort me" (Psalm 23:4). This corollary truth, of his walking with us, is also so necessary for us to understand that it is repeated over and over again in scripture.

Isaiah put the Lord's promise into inspiring poetry: "I have called thee by thy name; thou art mine. When thou passest through the waters, I will be with thee; and through the rivers, they shall not overflow thee: when thou walkest through the fire, thou shalt not be burned; neither shall the flame kindle upon thee. For I am the Lord thy God. . . . Thou wast precious in my sight . . . and I have loved thee" (Isaiah 43:1-4). The Lord knows us by name! We are precious to him! He will walk through our fiery trials with us!

Illustrating this poetic truth, we are given the story of Shadrach, Meshach, and Abed-nego. In their story we receive a visual image of the principle we are examining. When the music plays, signaling the people to bow before Nebuchadnezzar's golden idol, the three Hebrew princes remain standing. The sentence of death is passed upon them, and they are "cast into the midst of the burning fiery furnace" (Daniel 3:21). True to Isaiah's promise, the Lord is with them. "Lo, I see four men loose, walking in the midst of the fire, and they have no hurt; and the form of the fourth is like the Son of God" (Daniel 3:25).

As is the case in many biblical stories, we are being shown in a dramatic visual way what the Lord will do for all of his children. The story of the three Hebrews is a grand symbol that illustrates exactly what Isaiah wrote. The Son of God will be with us in our trials. We may walk through the fire of adversity, the waters may pass over our heads, the storms may rage against us, but One walks with us, sharing our burden, protecting us that we may "have no hurt." The story of Shadrach, Meshach, and Abed-nego is replayed over and over again throughout the world. I have seen it in my life and in the lives of others. As a boy I wanted to witness such marvels and wondered why they did not continue to happen, but in time I understood. The crucial point of the story is not the final outcome of our fiery furnace moments but the assurance that we do not face them alone.

God assures us in the book of Isaiah that his empathy and understanding are incomparable: "To whom will ye liken me, and make me equal, and compare me?" (Isaiah 46:5). "Even to your old age I am he; and even to hoar hairs will I carry you: I have made, and I will bear; even I will carry, and will deliver you" (Isaiah 46:4). These promises do not mean we will not experience adversity or that we will not suffer through its stinging pain. We are assured that it is better to pass through sorrow, but sorrow will not leave an eternal mark on our souls except for good. Isaiah's words are correct: there is no God like our God, one who feels all that we feel and guides us through our oppositions, assuring us he can turn them all to our good. So that all human experience might be encompassed in his understanding, Jesus "descended below all things, in that he comprehended all things, that he might be in all and through all things" (D&C 88:6).

Joseph Smith was comforted by this truth during those long months in Liberty Jail. "The Son of Man hath descended below them all," the Lord told Joseph (D&C 122:8). There is no sorrow, pain, temptation, trial, affliction, grief, or adversity he does not understand. In truth he comprehends them at their deepest level. And he was the best of men.

It is always a blessing when we have friends to see us through our challenges, but if we are not favored with such strengthening associations, if we have to face our adversities alone, we know there is One who walks with us. We can testify as did Paul, writing to Timothy when the sentence of death was about to be pronounced upon him: "At my first answer no man stood with me, but all men forsook me: . . . Notwithstanding the Lord stood with me, and strengthened me . . . and I was delivered out of the mouth of the lion" (2 Timothy 4:16–17).

CHAPTER SEVEN

—⁓—

The Lord is good unto them that wait
for him, to the soul that seeketh him. It is good
that a man should both hope and quietly
wait for the salvation of the Lord.

Lamentations 3:25–26

IN THE DAYS WHEN THE JUDGES RULED

"Did Heaven Look On?"

This is all fine and glorious, we might say, but there are pains
and suffering on the earth that are difficult to justify in anyone's
faith, particularly a faith that presupposes a loving God, depicted as
a Father—and an all-powerful one, too. Can all the promised good,
can even the knowledge that God himself suffered more than anyone else, make up for the intensity of human suffering? Men have
wrestled with this question from the very beginning. Shakespeare,
in particular, poses the question in a number of his plays. When
Macduff hears that Macbeth has slaughtered his wife and children,
he cries: "Did Heaven look on and would not take their part?"[1] In
Richard the Third, Elizabeth, upon hearing that Richard has killed
her two young sons, demands of God an accounting of what he has
allowed to happen. "Wilt thou, O God, fly from such gentle lambs
and throw them in the entrails of the wolf? When didst thou sleep,

when such a deed was done?"[2] Even Juliet in her despair cries to the heavens, which are supposed to be filled with the compassion of God: "Is there no pity sitting in the clouds that sees into the bottom of my grief. . . . Alack, alack, that Heaven should practice stratagems upon so soft a subject as myself!"[3]

We often answer these cries with the argument of agency. God has given man his agency, which means that some use their agency to inflict pain on others. There is truth in this argument, but it seems inadequate. If I as a father were to allow one of my children to torture, abuse, inflict pain or intense suffering upon another of my children, and I did nothing to stop it, all would condemn me. If I gave as my reason for not interceding, "They must be free to choose. They have their agency," the hollowness of that statement would echo into empty space. No moral, ethical system on earth would sanction this, would it? God must be more just than man—his system of morality higher, his ethic purer. Agency cannot fully answer Macduff's cry. Is there anything that can?

We are entering into a shadowland where human wisdom is dim. We are back with Job on the ash heap, wondering why God would allow such things. We are with the children in the world's concentration camps, looking for God in a world of gas and ovens. We are with Joseph in Liberty Jail, asking, "Where art thou?" (D&C 121:1).

There is some comfort when we struggle with such things in knowing that some of the greatest souls and minds in the scriptures also wrestled to understand. "Shall not the Judge of all the earth do right?" Abraham questioned (Genesis 18:25). That is a bold question to ask of God. Others have been equally bold. For those who believe in a loving, all-powerful God, the question simply will not go away. It is adversity's most potent blow at faith and theism's perennial problem. The heart of the dilemma is, perhaps, no more lovingly stated than when we hear Primary children sing, "Heavenly Father, are you really there? And do you hear and answer ev'ry child's prayer?"[4] The suffering of children is so difficult to justify in a universe overflowing with compassion such as Enoch experienced. The scriptures tell us what we should do in such a world.

The Ugliest Chapters in Scripture

So much of what we read in the scriptures is edifying. The stories that are related and the examples given match the description we read of in the thirteenth article of faith. They are virtuous, lovely, praiseworthy and of good report. We delight in reading them and leave refreshed. And yet there are areas in the scriptures where the feeling we receive from reading is not the emotional, spiritual, almost musical, lift so dominant in most chapters. I have at times asked my students, "What are the ugliest chapters in scripture?" I usually do not get an answer. Occasionally one will say, "Moroni 9," which has some very disturbing things recorded. They are right in that assessment. Moroni 9 records some brutal and perverted actions by the warring parties. But the chapters I am looking for when I ask this question are Judges 19 through 21. I cannot think of a section of scripture that contains more inhumane and insane actions than the end of Judges. Earlier in my career, I refused to teach that section, but I finally decided I should try to understand why those stories were allowed to remain in sacred writ. A brief recital of some of the events might be useful.

We are introduced to a Levite and his concubine. She runs away from her husband and returns to her father's house. Depending on how one reads the description of the wife, the reason for her running may have been her own adulterous behavior. The Levite goes after her and effects reconciliation.

On their journey home they are obliged to seek shelter for the night. Hesitant to stay overnight in a Canaanite village, the couple stop in a village belonging to the tribe of Benjamin. Here they find accommodations with an old man. But certain young men of the city abuse the Levite's wife during the night so badly that she dies in the morning at the threshold of the door, which is described with great poignancy.

To unite the tribes against Benjamin, the Levite divides her body and sends it to the other eleven tribes. This succeeds in getting their attention, and they demand the perpetrators of the assault and murder. In a show of tribal pride and autonomy, the Benjamites refuse to deliver up the young men for execution.

This launches a civil war between Benjamin and the other tribes. They slaughter each other in battle after battle, including entire populations, men, women, and children. Villages are burned, and even the animals are destroyed. Finally Benjamin is decimated. Only six hundred men remain.

Realizing they have almost totally annihilated one of the twelve tribes of Israel, the other eleven tribes cease fighting and arrange a treaty. With all the Benjamite women killed, a problem arises. The men of the other tribes have sworn an oath that they would not give their daughters in marriage to any Benjamite man. How can they, then, populate the tribe of Benjamin? They decide to kill all the people of Jabesh-Gilead because they had not sworn an oath to God at Mizpeh. The people of Jabesh-Gilead are slaughtered, except for the young women, who are given to the men of Benjamin for wives. Unfortunately, there are not enough.

"The elders of the congregation" (Judges 21:16) tell the remaining

Benjamite men to kidnap the daughters of Shiloh, an Israelite settlement, while the rest of the people of Shiloh are celebrating a feast to the Lord. In this way no one will break their oath by actually giving his daughter as a bride. The hypocrisy of honoring an oath to the Lord by committing murder is more than ironic.

The world described in Judges is a brutal, unforgiving, arrogant, and perverted world. I used to wonder why these chapters were still in the canon. Surely some prophetic editor should have stricken out those stories long ago. The sad state of affairs recounted in Judges 19–21 is preceded by the story of Samson, who, though physically strong, becomes morally corrupt and completely selfish. He dies with the Philistines because he has become, essentially, one of them in behavior.

Judges ends with a succinct description of the world at that time: "Every man did that which was right in his own eyes" (Judges 21:25). It is a world where anything goes, where the credo is "Every man for himself!" Few rules apply, and those that do are upside down. It is a world where keeping an oath has a higher value than punishing those who kidnap, rape, or murder. I dislike even recounting the distasteful and ugly tale.

I was once pondering this section, asking again why it was included in scripture, when I received the insight I needed: "This is the world you live in! Do you not recognize it?" That insight stunned me. Surveying recent history, including the Holocaust, Soviet purges, genocides in Cambodia, Kosovo, Rwanda, Sudan, and a dozen other places where human-inflicted suffering on a massive scale was (and is) endured, proves the point. We live in a world where airplanes are flown into buildings, a world where violent pornography proliferates, child abuse multiplies, "ethnic cleansing" has become a euphemism for genocide, starvation occurs even in

the most affluent countries, mass murders are carrie
and on college campuses, and multiple other examp
vengeance, perversion, and brutality cry to us from th
It is a sad commentary that much of what is considere
tertainment centers on such aspects of life and that the
for gratifying the worst elements of the natural man i
that the media is simply a mirror of reality.

Such events cause us, especially those whose lives
by them, to question how God can allow such things. I
to agency is not sufficient, what are we to think? What ar

Giving Dignity and Humanity to the Huma

Sometimes the Lord teaches powerful truths in the
by contrasting certain stories with each other. In literatu
sometimes referred to as using a "foil." The contrast creates
sage. After all the hate and destruction of Judges, what is
next story in the Bible? It is Ruth! Ruth begins with a des
of the world *she* lived in: "Now it came to pass in the days w
judges ruled" (Ruth 1:1). If I were to choose the most be
book or story in the Old Testament, it would be the book o
Its flavor is reminiscent of the Gospels, especially that of Luk
three central characters are grandly selfless. The only nonexer
moment is provided by Ruth's near kinsman, who is afraid he
"mar [his] own inheritance" (Ruth 4:6). Ruth is only conce
about Naomi, and Naomi seeks only the happiness of Ruth.
blesses them both. The book of Ruth is the most polite of all b
of the Bible. Everyone is well-mannered and gentle; everyor
kind. Ruth saves part of the meal that Boaz gives her for Nac
who would not have eaten that day; Boaz instructs his young n
to drop grain purposely for Ruth that her gleaning may be eas

ne cannot but love these three simple and wonderful people. There is nothing grand or historically significant about the story of Ruth. There are no heroic actions, no great discourses, no battles won or lost, no obstacles surmounted, no kings or warriors. We are introduced to three people whose love for and devotion to each other are manifested in the simplest of ways.

When I finish reading Judges, I am weary of mind and sore of soul. I do not wish to belong to a race of men who do such things to each other. How can they be the children of God? How can they even be the creations of God? I feel this same way at times when I watch the evening news and hear of some act of terrorism abroad or a mass killing at home. In my personal scripture study I used to stop after reading Judges because I had come to the end of a book, but I never do now. I always continue reading until I have finished Ruth. There is healing in the story. The balm of selfless love flows over my heart, and I feel calm. I want to belong to a race that can produce such people. I can believe God is their Father and their Creator.

These two sections of scripture were placed side by side that we might view our own world through the contrasting lens of both experiences. I must believe—and I know that this is true—that there are men and women all over this sad planet who act toward each other just as Naomi, Ruth, and Boaz did. We may not hear of their simple acts of kindness and love, but they are accomplished by the tens of thousands every day. I have met Ruths and Naomis in the modern world. I assume you have also. They give dignity and nobility to the human race and atone in a measure for the brutality and suffering of mankind. Can their combined mass in the scale of humanity counterbalance the combined evil and cruelty of others? Perhaps not, but the weight of their example can counterbalance our

despair. They can show us a way to live and to be. We need not despair, wringing our hands over the insanities of the world. We know the work we must do, and we go out and do it. If we fail, we give the world over to its lowest common denominator.

The story of Ruth does not answer the questions posed by Shakespeare's characters, but I find direction and hope in it. There is no question about what we are to do if we find ourselves in a world similar to that described in the final chapters of Judges. We must love. We must learn to be gentle. We must be kind. We must forgive. In the tiny daily acts of life, we must provide the balance that gives meaning to life and, though it is not a full answer to human suffering, may be the only answer we can offer. If we find it difficult to explain the cruelty of man, we have by way of a counterbalance the great goodness of man. Where does Ruth-like nobility and kindness come from? What is the source of such selfless compassion? Herein we find a compelling argument for God. There must be a source of all this wholesome gentility. If the evils of the world argue against our faith in God, then purity, goodness, patience, charity, and the unadorned simple kindnesses and mercies of mankind lead us to another conclusion.

One of my favorite Russian novels is *The Brothers Karamazov*. Dostoevsky tells the story of three brothers and their various approaches to life. Mitya, irresponsible but likeable, is devoted to enjoying life. Ivan, the intellectual, broods over the major questions of life, especially the question of God and suffering. Alyosha, one of the most beautiful characters in modern literature, is Dostoevsky's hero, a Russian Orthodox novice whose pure love penetrates right to the core of his soul. In one of the central encounters of the novel, Ivan relates stories of the suffering of children to Alyosha. They are painful to hear, and the questions they bring, of whether God exists, if he truly is goodness and love, knock loudly on the door of faith. Ivan concludes that no earthly or heavenly good can offset the suffering of one child:

"'Tell me,' Ivan says, 'I challenge you—reply: imagine that you yourself are erecting the edifice of human fortune with the goal of, at the finale, making people happy, of at last giving them peace and quiet, but that in order to do it it would be necessary and unavoidable to torture to death only one tiny little creature, that same little child that beat its breast with its little fist, and on its unavenged tears to found that edifice, would you agree to be the architect on those conditions, tell me and tell me truly?'"[5]

How can any of us answer Ivan's question? Alyosha takes his cue from his own heart and from a story Ivan has told him about Christ before the Grand Inquisitor. He rises, and kisses his brother with forgiving, compassionate understanding—with the full measure of his perfect soul. In Dostoevsky's creation, love is the only answer one can offer. It is Ruth's answer to the world of Judges. It is an answer based on action, not on philosophy, on what we can do, not on what we know or do not know about God. "'What is hell?'" Dostoevsky writes. "'The suffering of no longer being able to love.'"[6]

When we cease loving, we deliver our world to an end-of-Judges fate where every man does that which is right in his own eyes. Ruth must and will prevail. I believe that is what Christ came to teach us. Part of his Atonement was to show us that we must love, even in the face of cruelty, injustice, violence, and brutality. In a world of adversity—adversity of the worst and most painful kind—let us answer as Jesus did, as Ruth and Naomi and Boaz did, as Alyosha did. Faith arises from such sacrifice and redeems the world.

Shakespeare, one of the most humane of writers, who challenged heaven with his questions, comes to the same conclusion. In

King Lear we are introduced to the same amorality that created the landscape depicted at the end of Judges and in Moroni 9. But all the ugliness of the play is redeemed in the final scenes with Lear and his daughter Cordelia. Here there is forgiveness and love and devotion and selfless sacrifice. "Upon such sacrifices, my Cordelia," Lear says, "the gods themselves throw incense."[7]

—ɯ—

To give unto them beauty for ashes,
the oil of joy for mourning, the garment of
praise for the spirit of heaviness.

Isaiah 61:3

Such As I Have

"Silver and Gold"

There are times we may feel helpless to end or even to alleviate
the suffering of others. There is a great deal of suffering in the
world, and those who are good naturally wish to do what they can
to bring relief and solace. I recall a time in my life when I was anxious about the happiness and welfare of individuals whom I love
very much. One wanted a baby and could not understand why God
would not send her a child. Another wanted the joy and compan-
ionship of an eternal marriage but felt the years passing and her
dreams dimming. Another, a dear friend, was struggling for the return of testimony. I recall spending many nights on my knees, as we
all have, pleading that the desired blessings or end of trials might
come. Surely the ram was in the thicket, but the trials continued.

It was at this stage of my life that a story in the book of Acts became profoundly beautiful to me and helped me as I related to the

struggles of those I loved. "A certain man lame from his mother's womb was carried, whom they laid daily at the gate of the temple which is called Beautiful, to ask alms of them that entered into the temple" (Acts 3:2). Later we are told that "the man was above forty years old" (Acts 4:22). This is an affliction of long duration, one we must suppose the man felt he would endure for a lifetime.

As Peter and John entered the temple, the man looked to them for alms. "And Peter, fastening his eyes upon him with John, said, Look on us. And he gave heed unto them, expecting to receive something of them. Then Peter said, Silver and gold have I none; but such as I have give I thee. In the name of Jesus Christ of Nazareth rise up and walk. And he took him by the right hand, and lifted him up" (Acts 3:4–7).

As I read this simple story with the needs of those I loved in mind, it imparted to me an essential insight. We can give only what we have. We should not feel inadequate or guilty because we cannot end the adversities of those we meet or of those we love, but that does not mean we have nothing to give. Peter and John did not have what the man at the gate of the temple anticipated, but they gave him what they had, which in this case was greater than the man expected. I did not have a child to give my friend; I did not have a husband I could provide my other friend; I did not have a store of faith I could inject into the soul of the friend who needed it. I could not give these things. I could give only what I had.

Perhaps you have felt similar frustrations or inadequacies. We can all give kindness. We can all give understanding. We can all listen. We can all give love, and often that is exactly what is most needed. We may yet, as Peter did, take someone by the right hand and lift them up.

I think of that lovely moment, misunderstood at first by Jesus' disciples, when Mary anointed the head and feet of the Savior. Sensing her Lord's life was nearing its end, Mary broke an alabaster box filled with precious ointment and anointed Jesus with it. When others in the room criticized Mary's act as wasteful, Jesus defended her, saying, "Why trouble ye her? she hath wrought a good work on me. . . . *She hath done what she could*" (Mark 14:6, 8; emphasis added). That is all we can do! For Jesus, what Mary had done was sufficient. It did not remove the thorns or the nails or the whip, but it was an act of lovingkindness that surely lifted the Savior's spirit as he felt the heaviness that would weigh down so pressingly in Gethsemane settle upon him. We all have our figurative alabaster boxes of ointment we can pour out. "She hath done what she could."

"Was Not the Giving Enough?"

Many years ago while I was directing the institute program in Boulder, Colorado, a young woman obviously in need came to my office. She was at least eight months pregnant, a tiny wisp of a girl about nineteen or twenty years of age. Her eyes darted back and forth, and I sensed she would flee like a rabbit at the slightest wrong move. She told me she had been sent to the Mormons because they would help her. She wanted her baby to be raised in a good home. She called me Reverend, and nothing I said would shake that title from her. In her mind, a reverend was safe. She was terrified of almost all other men.

I took her home to my wife and thus started a process of helping her to heal. One traumatic night, when we tried to convince her to let a doctor see her because her delivery was near, we discovered what had happened in her past to create in her the perpetual sense of fear and distrust. As a child she had been abused by her father.

When she was old enough, she ran away from home to another state where she found a job, rented an apartment, and began a new life. But fortune was not kind to her. One night while returning home late from getting a pizza, she was attacked by two men underneath a burned-out street lamp. Her relating this account was one of the most painful events I have experienced in my life. It stirred within me the old question of *Why?* Why would God allow such a painful and harrowing event in the life of a young woman already traumatized by an unhappy and abusive childhood?

Hearing her account of her past caused us to be all the more desirous of helping her. She was easy to love, and events began to line up for her future. A wonderful young couple who were having trouble having children would take the baby into their family. Funds were provided for her to receive university schooling. She was being counseled by concerned and professional counselors from LDS Social Services. Everything was going well, but we did not see all that was going on in her mind. One morning she told us she was going to take a walk. She went out the front door, walked to the bus stop, and boarded a bus. We never saw her again.

I was devastated, consumed with worry about her and the still unborn baby. I wanted a happy ending. My expectation was that this young woman's story would end positively. How could it have concluded in mystery and uncertainty? The counselors from LDS Social Services tried to explain that sometimes people who have been denied love and have suffered traumatic memories find it difficult to feel and express love when it is truly offered. They fear it will be taken away, or they sense that they cannot return love without making themselves vulnerable. As a result, they simply shut down their hearts and turn away. This explanation was not satisfying for me, although I understood it. In my frustration with our failure to change her life and provide a decent life for her child, I turned my thoughts heavenward, but not in faith. I found myself avoiding God, because I was angry with him for permitting this young woman to leave. Couldn't she have stayed at least long enough for us to provide for her child? Though I did not confront the Lord directly, those emotions and thoughts were in my heart. For days I tried to pray around them, but inwardly I was crying, "O God, where art thou?" and "Righteous art thou, O Lord . . . yet let me talk with thee of thy judgments" (D&C 121:1; Jeremiah 12:1).

This serious form of hide-and-seek with God continued for several weeks. I suppose the Lord was waiting for me to approach him, but I kept everything bottled up inside. How can one be angry at the Lord and refuse to deal with the guilt that is associated with those thoughts? And I was angry. In time the still, small voice penetrated the wall I had built up. I remembered that the Lord knew what was in my heart. Why shouldn't I pour it out? I thought of Hannah and her interaction with God when she wanted a child: "I am a woman of a sorrowful spirit" she said, "but have poured out my soul before the Lord. . . . Out of the abundance of my complaint and grief have I spoken" (1 Samuel 1:15–16). The example of Hannah gave me courage and the assurance that one can respectfully complain to God. Sometimes it is best to just pour it out.

"Why did it have to end the way it did?" I asked. "Where were You? Couldn't You have kept her here at least long enough for the baby to be taken care of? Now she is gone and who knows what life they both are going into." As my emotions surfaced, I wasn't even respectful enough to use the proper language of prayer. The Lord is patient, though, and, as we have seen, he understands "according to the flesh" all that we pass through (Alma 7:12). When I was finished, the Spirit gave me an answer: "That which you have done is not lost. Did you need an answer for your love? Was not the giving enough?"

"According to the Love of God in Me"

We will not always see the fruition of our efforts in helping others through the adversities of their lives. We may not receive the desired endings, but love itself is an answer, and in God's eternal economy, no act of love or selflessness or kindness will ever be lost. I think of such men as Mormon and Moroni and Noah who, hoping to turn their people around, preached for years, only to see them sink deeper and deeper into misery and destruction. I cannot doubt in the least as I read Mormon's words that he deeply loved his people:

"When I . . . saw their lamentation and their mourning and their sorrow before the Lord, my heart did begin to rejoice within me, knowing the mercies and the long-suffering of the Lord. . . . But behold this my joy was vain, for their sorrowing was not unto repentance . . . it was rather the sorrowing of the damned, because the Lord would not always suffer them to take happiness in sin. . . . My sorrow did return unto me again" (Mormon 2:12-14, 15).

In a later entry in the scriptural record Mormon spoke of his love: "I had led them . . . and had loved them, according to the love of God which was in me, with all my heart; and my soul had been poured out in prayer unto my God all the day long for them" (Mormon 3:12). This love would be most eloquently expressed from the summit of the Hill Cumorah as he surveyed the scene of destruction below him. "O ye fair ones," he lamented. "Ye are gone, and my sorrows cannot bring your return" (Mormon 6:17, 20).

Yet even Mormon could not, would not, relinquish eternal

hope for his people. "But behold, ye are gone, and the Father, yea, the Eternal Father of heaven, knoweth your state; and he doeth with you according to his justice and mercy" (Mormon 6:22). These words echo in my mind when I think of the fearful young woman who walked into the institute in Boulder, Colorado, one day and then into our lives and hearts. Did not Jesus tell the multitude at Bountiful when he told them he had to visit the lost tribes of Israel, "They are not lost unto the Father, for he knoweth whither he hath taken them"? (3 Nephi 17:4). Surely in the eternal time of our Father in Heaven nothing is lost. Until all becomes clear, we have our assignment: love and give, leaving the rest in the Lord's hands, assured that one day, somehow, none will be lost even in the most desperate of cases. Herein is our hope and our answer.

CHAPTER NINE

—∿—

Look down from heaven . . . where is thy zeal and
thy strength, the sounding of thy bowels and of thy
mercies toward me? are they restrained?

Isaiah 63:15

SUFFICIENT UNTO THE DAY

Returning to Jerusalem

If there are times when we cannot lift the burden, prevent the
adversity, or end the sorrow of others or ourselves, there are also
times when we place upon ourselves burdens whose weight we were
never meant to carry. This happens most often when we bear the
load of a whole lifetime of adversity at once. Sometimes in the midst
of a present crisis, challenge, or disappointment we reflect on the
past, bringing back former defeats. Then, not content with dealing
with only the present and the past, we project the worst of scenar-
ios into the future. Suddenly the soul is bearing a load too heavy for
it. We must learn to stay in the present when dealing with adversity.
The past is over and cannot be changed—we must learn from it and
let it go. The future has not yet come; experience tells us that more
often than not our worst fears do not materialize. Though they did
for Job, they need not for us. We can prepare for the future to a

certain extent, but we cannot control it as we often desire. When future setbacks come, we will deal with them; by that time the present distress will be in the past. We must remember we do not have to face an accumulation of sorrows. When we do so, we break the spirit and resiliency of life. Jesus taught, "Take therefore no thought for the morrow: for the morrow shall take thought for the things of itself. Sufficient unto the day is the evil thereof" (Matthew 6:34).

A perfect example of this teaching is found in the Book of Mormon. While traveling in the wilderness toward the land of Bountiful, Lehi's family endured many hardships, but the death of Ishmael precipitated a crisis for the family. "And it came to pass that the daughters of Ishmael did mourn exceedingly, because of the loss of their father" (1 Nephi 16:35). This was a present source of adversity. It is natural to mourn the passing of a parent, and we might conclude that Ishmael's passing was in the eyes of his daughters premature, a result of years in the wilderness. Notice, however, how the daughters of Ishmael add the past to their present difficulties and then project negatively into the future:

"They did murmur against my father, because he had brought them out of the land of Jerusalem, saying: Our father is dead [present]; yea, and we have wandered much in the wilderness, and we have suffered much affliction, hunger, thirst, and fatigue [past]; and after all these sufferings we must perish in the wilderness with hunger [future]" (1 Nephi 16:35). In the future they are not going to perish; they will obtain a promised land, although future challenges still await them.

The net result of carrying the adversity of the past, present, and future all at once is usually the desire to give up. The load is simply too great. "And thus they did murmur against my father, and also against me; and they were desirous to return again to Jerusalem"

(1 Nephi 16:36). We all know that feeling. From time to time we all want to return to Jerusalem. This return may take many forms. Perhaps we are struggling in a marriage. It is the most natural thing in the world to look back to the past and vividly remember mismanagements or arguments. It is also very human to say as we ponder the future, "He (or she) will never change." Missionaries face a similar dilemma. They lose a great contact, think of contacts they have lost in the past, and anticipate, "I will never see anyone baptized." I have seen this scenario played out many times in college as students face difficult classes. I have seen it while serving in Church leadership and trying to help people with the problems of their lives. We all do this. It is important that we learn from the past. We do not wish to obliterate our memories, as they contain helpful lessons. We do not wish to blindly plunge into the future, either. The present is the only thing we can do something about. Here we must focus our energy.

If we need a further example from the Book of Mormon, we find one in Sariah's comments to Lehi when their sons do not return as quickly as she expects from their attempt to bring the plates of brass back to their camp in the wilderness. "My mother, Sariah, was exceedingly glad, for she truly had mourned because of us." Hers was an unnecessary mourning, though a very natural expression of anxiety. "For she had supposed that we had perished in the wilderness; and she also had complained against my father . . . saying: Behold thou hast led us forth from the land of our inheritance, and my sons are no more, and we perish in the wilderness" (1 Nephi 5:1–2).

As in the case with the daughters of Ishmael the worst is anticipated. There is a better way, and the scriptures reveal it to us.

"Bear with Patience"

When each of my children prepares to depart on his or her mission, the last advice I give is the sharing of a verse from the Book of Mormon. It is the one verse about missionary life I want each of them to etch indelibly into their consciousness. We could make a fairly good case that the sons of Mosiah were some of the most powerful missionaries in scripture. The stories of Ammon, Aaron, Lamoni, Lamoni's father, Abish, the Anti-Nephi-Lehis, and others are legendary. The success of the four sons was beyond their expectations, and to this day our own missionary program is largely established on the principles we learn from studying the years they spent with the Lamanites. Yet even these inspired, focused, and highly successful men faced adversity. Here is the verse I share with my children, wanting them to know that even the best had their tough moments. I feel it provides a type of scriptural armor for future discouraging moments that surely come in the life of all missionaries.

"Now when our hearts were depressed, and we were about to turn back, behold, the Lord comforted us, and said: Go amongst thy brethren, the Lamanites, and bear with patience thine afflictions, and I will give unto you success" (Alma 26:27).

What is true of missionary experiences is also true in other areas of our lives. Sometimes we want to turn back because our hearts are depressed. This happened to the very best and most devoted of the Lord's servants. The answer, the comfort the Lord offers, is two-fold. First, he recommends patience. I think it interesting that the verb the Lord chooses is *bear*. That word suggests that he knows patience is not always the easiest quality to acquire. He does not minimize the challenges. He acknowledges the heavy weight some are obliged to carry for a time. Second, the Lord promises future success. Here the turning of one's mind to the future is a positive turning rather than a negative one. We cannot emphasize too greatly the need to follow this line of thinking. That is often hard to do because it seems natural to follow the daughters of Ishmael and anticipate the worst. When one has experienced a long string of adversities that have worn down one's soul, as the daughters of Ishmael had, it is difficult not to project difficulty into the future. Yet positive projection into the future is what the Lord recommends while we patiently bear the present distress. In time the blessings that came to the sons of Mosiah outweighed their afflictions. Ammon summarizes that period of his life with these remarkable words: "Yea, I say unto you, there never were men that had so great reason to rejoice as we, since the world began" (Alma 26:35). That is a long cry from the discouragement and depression that tempted them all to turn back.

"He Prayed More Earnestly"

During those times when we carry a lifetime of worry and distress, the will to continue ceases, and far too frequently we abandon ourselves to our adversity with feelings of hopelessness. We think, What can I do but submit? The temptation to capitulate can also come after a long battle with a particular adversity. The sheer longevity of the conflict wears one down. Yet the scriptures tell us it is at this time precisely that we must turn with our greatest energy toward God, and we may expect help. In the Sacred Grove, as Joseph Smith battled with an unseen power, he reached the point of despair. "But, exerting all my powers to call upon God to deliver me out of the power of this enemy which had seized upon me, and at the very moment when *I was ready to sink into despair and abandon myself* to destruction . . . just at this moment of great alarm, I saw a pillar of light" (Joseph Smith-History 1:16; emphasis added). The promised relief finally comes.

Let us also remember the Lord's final words to Joseph in Liberty Jail: "Hold on thy way." That is not a bad motto for life regardless of what we are facing. Let us continue our course as best we can, and let us hold on, "for God shall be with you forever and ever." There is additional comfort in the words "their bounds are set, they cannot pass" (D&C 122:9). There are limits! Our strength will be sufficient within those limits if we avoid the mistake of the daughters of Ishmael and deal only with our present adversity. I believe with all my heart that the Lord will not allow our adversity to pass those limits. Did not Paul promise, "There hath no temptation taken you but such as is common to man: but God is faithful, who will not suffer you to be tempted above that ye are able; but will with the temptation also make a way to escape, that ye may be able to bear it"? (1 Corinthians 10:13). Temptation in this context means more than enticement to disobedience; rather, it encompasses the idea of trials and adversity in general.

When Moses faced a similar challenge in his own individual combat with the adversary, he too called upon God. There is a very interesting shift of wording in Moses' account. First we read, "Moses began to fear exceedingly. . . . Nevertheless, calling upon God, he received strength" (Moses 1:20). Notice the order—first, prayer, and then strength is given! Praying intensely brings the desired strength. Yet even that was not sufficient for Moses' confrontation. The adversary does not leave. In the next verse the order is reversed: "And Moses received strength, and called upon God" (Moses 1:21). Here the order is first strength and then prayer! There may be times in our lives when the answer the Lord gives to our fervent prayers is the strength to pray even more ardently. God helps us to call upon him with the energy we lack, an energy that may be depleted because of our long battle. Perhaps that is what Paul meant when he told the Romans, "The Spirit also helpeth our infirmities: for we know not what we should pray for as we ought: but the Spirit itself maketh intercession for us with groanings which cannot be uttered" (Romans 8:26).

The supreme example of this principle is found in the New Testament during Christ's hours in Gethsemane. Only Luke records the details: "And there appeared an angel unto him from heaven, strengthening him. And being in an agony he prayed more earnestly" (Luke 22:43-44). I think it interesting that the strengthening angel was not sufficient. Here was a friend of friends, a powerful one, one sent from the Father himself, but even an angel could not alleviate nor lessen the agony sufficiently. Jesus' only recourse was to pray "more earnestly."

I sense in this earnest praying more than the expectation for an answer. I suppose that most of the time when I pray, I anticipate an answer. But this prayer seems to be a prayer sufficient in itself, expecting no answer, but simply a prayer that helps one endure—not because something is granted, but because the very act of praying at that level is necessary and produces an enduring power. Exerting all our power to call upon God may be the answer itself. The ability to exert all our power, though lacking in ourselves, may be supplied by a concerned Father in Heaven.

Let us examine Hannah's particular prayer more intently. Hannah faced the trial of being childless and in addition had to endure the taunts of the other wife, Peninnah, who "provoked her sore, for to make her fret" (1 Samuel 1:6). She turned to the Lord for solace. I love the description of how she prayed. "She was in bitterness of soul," we read (1 Samuel 1:10). "I am a woman of a sorrowful spirit: I have . . . poured out my soul before the Lord. . . . Out of the abundance of my complaint and grief have I spoken hitherto" (1 Samuel 1:15–16). We pour out whatever is in us, our complaints, certainly our sorrows, even our bitterness and our frets.

We saw that Moses and Elijah, when they wanted to give up, openly poured out their complaints before God. Joseph Smith poured out his anxieties in a similar manner in that pleading prayer from Liberty Jail which begins Doctrine and Covenants 121. It is not difficult to describe their prayers as complaints, born of frustration and long experience dealing with rebellious and difficult people or the continual depredations of the mobs. There is comfort in the knowledge that God's dignity can handle our complaints, that we do not need to feel guilty because our prayers might take the form of complaints. What better thing is there to do with bitterness of soul than to empty it out of ourselves? And who better to bear this emptying than the One Being we know can handle it?

It is important to read the result of this pouring out for Hannah. "So the woman went her way, and did eat, and her countenance was no more sad" (1 Samuel 1:18). Rather than living in the unfocused world of the past and future, let us pray more earnestly, let us pour out all that is within us and depart with hope in our countenances.

Lingering in the Valley of Sorrow

One of my most beloved passages in the Book of Mormon is Nephi's psalm, recorded in 2 Nephi 4. I love this passage for its sheer poetic beauty, its honesty of heart, and its rhythmic lift, but also because I see a very good man mourning over his inability to live the way he desires. He too is "encompassed about, because of the temptations and the sins which do so easily beset me" (2 Nephi

4:18). We can relate to this man. "O wretched man that I am!" he exclaims (2 Nephi 4:17). Though there may be poetic drama in his words, we cannot doubt the sincerity of his feelings. This chapter in 2 Nephi carries the same power to bind us to a scriptural personality as Joseph Smith's words before his first visit from Moroni: "I often felt condemned for my weakness and imperfections. . . . I betook myself to prayer" (Joseph Smith–History 1:29).

The context of Nephi's hymn is the death of his father, Lehi, and the coming separation of Lehi's family at the crisis Lehi's death will bring. In this section of the Book of Mormon we are invited to examine how Nephi deals with the death of his father compared to the way the daughters of Ishmael deal with the death of theirs. What has held Lehi's family together is Lehi. When he dies, the point of contention that has plagued his family from the first—that of leadership—must be resolved. Nephi senses it will end in total alienation. He is angered by his brothers' squabbling and saddened to the point of depression over his life circumstances. He uses an enlightening word to describe his situation: "Why should my heart weep and my soul *linger* in the valley of sorrow, and my flesh waste away, and my strength slacken, because of mine afflictions?" (2 Nephi 4:26; emphasis added). That is a remarkably accurate description of how we all feel in times of intense adversity and, to a lesser extent, perhaps, in trials of lesser intensity. The key word for our consideration is *linger*. *Waste* and *slacken* are also worthy of our consideration.

We all will enter the valley of sorrow during our lives, undoubtedly many times, but we must not linger there. We must traverse it and walk out of its shadow, but it is tempting to let the flesh waste away in solitary self-pity, to let our strength slacken in apathy. In an ironic way there is a certain pleasure in self-pity and depression.

There is a relief, both an emotional and a physical relief, in wasting and slackening. That relief comes when we feel we will no longer fight. Struggling requires energy, and there is a kind of rest when we give in. I know these feelings as well as any. But we must try hard not to give in. I return to the Lord's suggestions to Moses, Elijah, and Joshua to *do something.* The very effort of walking out of the valley is healing. We will not linger. We will not slacken. In some respects Nephi at this juncture was doing what the daughters of Ishmael had done earlier, but in his case we learn an additional lesson.

It is all right to reflect upon the past so long as we know which memories to bring to the surface. The daughters of Ishmael reviewed the negatives, the past miseries. In Nephi's psalm he does just the opposite. That makes all the difference. Rather than desiring to give up, he is invigorated and enlivened by his journey through the past:

"My God hath been my support; he hath led me through mine afflictions in the wilderness. . . . He hath filled me with his love, even unto the consuming of my flesh. . . . Upon the wings of his Spirit hath my body been carried away . . . and mine eyes have beheld great things. . . . O then, if I have seen so great things, if the Lord in his condescension unto the children of men hath visited men in so much mercy, why should my heart weep?" (2 Nephi 4:20-21, 25-26).

He has walked out of the valley of sorrow by walking the road of his own memories. We sometimes call this counting our blessings, but this is something deeper. If there do not seem to be many blessings to rejoice over in the present, there will surely be those of the past. In Nephi's case, the past becomes a source of hope for the future rather than cause for despair. "I have trusted in thee, and I will

trust in thee forever" (2 Nephi 4:34). How much better use of the
past and future this is than that shown by the daughters of Ishmael.
If we are going to return to the past, let us return to positive memories. If we are going to project into the future, let us see it through
the lens of happy memories of our blessings, not our present
difficulties.

Optimism may not always come through. Sometimes we will
have to wait and see, but optimism will make the present bearable.
By focusing on our blessings and happy memories, we will not want
to return to Jerusalem or desire to turn back and thus miss the success that may await us around the corner. As Elizabeth Bennett tells
Mr. Darcy in Jane Austen's *Pride and Prejudice,* "You must learn
some of my philosophy. Think only of the past as its remembrance
gives you pleasure."[1]

"All These Things Are Against Me"

We gain further insight from Jacob, son of Isaac, into how difficult it is to read the future correctly. Here is a man who knew something of adversity. He is separated from his family because of his
conflict with his brother, Esau, and remains away from them for
twenty years. He faces conflicts between his wives Leah and Rachel.
He is deceived by his father-in-law, Laban, both in his marriage to
Leah and also when working with his flocks. His beloved wife,
Rachel, dies giving birth to her second son, Benjamin. His oldest
son sleeps with one of his wives. His other sons are far from righteous, from the selling of Joseph into slavery, to Judah's marriage
with a Canaanite and his easy morality, to Simeon and Levi's cruelty in slaughtering the men of Shechem's village. His daughter
Dinah is kidnapped and raped. His righteous and beloved son

Joseph is, as far as he knows, dead, and then his family faces starvation in the famine. This is a man who knows adversity.

There are two times in Jacob's life when he reads the present and the future incorrectly. Both are worthy of examination.

First, having run from the anger of his brother, Esau, Jacob spends twenty years serving Laban. After twenty years, things are not going well, however, and Jacob, having counseled with both the Lord and his wives, decides it is time to return home. His mother, Rebekah, had indicated to him when he first left for his uncle's home that his estrangement with Esau need not be long: "Tarry with him *a few days,* until thy brother's fury turn away" (Genesis 27:44; emphasis added). Jacob returns with anxiety to the land of his nativity.

When he hears that Esau is on the way to meet him with four hundred men, he assumes the worst, believing that Esau is coming to kill him. "Then Jacob was greatly afraid and distressed" (Genesis 32:7). Having left Laban secretly, Jacob has already burned his bridges back to his father-in-law. He cannot return to Haran, and he has been told by the Lord to go to Canaan. It is forward or nothing. He divides his caravan in two, hoping one can escape if the other is destroyed. He then pours out his fears to the Lord:

"Deliver me, I pray thee, from the hand of my brother, from the hand of Esau: for I fear him, lest he will come and smite me, and the mother with the children." His opinion of Esau is not very high; he assumes his brother will not only kill him but also his women and children. He reminds the Lord of past promises: "Thou saidst, I will surely do thee good, and make thy seed as the sand of the sea" (Genesis 32:11–12).

Hoping to appease his assumed vengeful brother, Jacob sends numerous flocks as gifts and then spends the night before he meets

Esau wrestling with God for a blessing. The anticipated encounter draws near. Placing himself before his wives and children, he "bowed himself to the ground seven times, until he came near to his brother." What will his reception be? What follows is one of the most endearing scenes in the Bible. "And Esau ran to meet him, and embraced him, and fell on his neck, and kissed him: and they wept" (Genesis 33:3–4). Next to (and foreshadowing) the prodigal son, this is the sweetest scene of forgiveness and reconciliation in scripture. It is on par with Joseph revealing himself to his brothers.

Jacob's fears were groundless. He was not going to meet a vengeful Esau but a tenderly forgiving brother. I can imagine the Lord thinking as Jacob poured out his fears to him: *You have no need to fear. Your prayers are already answered. Meeting your brother holds nothing but beauty.*

Many times our worst fears have no basis in reality, but only the passage of time will tell us that. In the meantime we fret and pour out our anxieties to an understanding God.

The second instance occurs later in Jacob's life, when he once again misreads a situation. If the story of Esau suggests Jacob's false reading of the future, the story of Benjamin represents an untrue interpretation of the present. As the famine dreamed of by Pharaoh and interpreted by Joseph increases, Jacob's ten sons travel to Egypt to buy food from the stores Joseph has accumulated. Joseph, recognizing his brothers and wanting to prove them, takes Simeon from them and demands that they return with their younger brother Benjamin.

As the famine continues and the necessity of a return trip to Egypt manifests itself, Jacob, fearful of losing Rachel's last son, tells his other sons, "Me have ye bereaved of my children: Joseph is not, and Simeon is not, and ye will take Benjamin away: *all these things are against me. . . .* Wherefore *dealt ye so ill with me,* as to tell the man whether ye had yet a brother?" (Genesis 42:36; 43:6; emphasis added).

Jacob's words are instructive in that nothing he says is actually true. Joseph is alive, a counselor to Pharaoh, and Jacob will soon be united with him. Simeon is also still alive, and Jacob will not lose Benjamin. Another beautiful forgiveness scene waits offstage! Perhaps the loss of Rachel had a profound effect on Jacob. In reality none of these things is against him. All are working for his salvation and that of his family. Soon even the famine, which he does not know will last seven years, will no longer be a concern for his survival. From an eternal perspective, no one has dealt ill with him—he just doesn't know it yet.

I do not think there is anyone alive who does not know by experience Jacob's way of thinking. We all misread events often. Time and faith heal these misconceptions. In light of this truth, I think it intriguing to ponder the blessing Jacob gives his sons Levi and Simeon. Levi and Simeon had slain all the males in the town where Shechem lived, because Shechem had defiled their sister Dinah. Jacob blessed them as follows: "Instruments of cruelty are in their habitations. O my soul, come not thou into their secret; . . . Cursed be their anger, for it was fierce. . . . I will divide them in Jacob, and scatter them in Israel" (Genesis 49:5–7).

This certainly sounds like a curse, but in the case of Levi it becomes a blessing. His descendants are the tribe to whom the Lord grants the priesthood. Rather than receiving a full territorial land inheritance when the tribes return from Egypt to inhabit the land of Canaan, the Levites are given villages scattered throughout the land, so that they might perform their priesthood functions for the whole house of Israel. The fulfillment of Jacob's words to Levi is positive, not negative.

Genesis ends with another case of seeing adversity when none existed. At Jacob's death, his other sons, still unable to fully accept Joseph's forgiveness and love, believe Joseph will now exact vengeance. What a testimony to the power of guilt and the human tendency to hold on to it! This story occurs four decades after they sold Joseph into slavery. The brothers concoct a story about Jacob's last words, purporting that they were for Joseph to forgive his brothers. This obvious fiction distresses Joseph, who had long ago forgiven his brothers. He weeps at their continued fears. Once again he reassures them that he holds no ill will toward them: "I will nourish you, and your little ones. And he comforted them, and spake kindly unto them" (Genesis 50:21).

Blessing or Bane

A story is told in China that illustrates these principles. The story comes from Taoist philosophy which, generally, hesitates to make many value judgments, seeing possibilities in all things and all experiences. The story projects a view of life that has seen the Chinese through centuries of hardship and is collected in a group of writings called the Huainanzi.

Near the northern borders of China was a man who lived his life according to the Taoist pattern. One day his mare wandered off and was lost in the territory of the Hu, northern tribes who were enemies to the Chinese. All of his neighbors offered him their sympathy.

"How unfortunate!" they said.

But the man was hesitant to pass judgment. He said, "Who

knows? Perhaps this will turn out to be a blessing. We will have to wait and see."

Within a few months, his mare returned and what is more, a fine horse from the northern territories accompanied her. Everyone now congratulated him. "How fortunate you are! You have an additional horse, a fine stallion!"

The man replied, "Perhaps, but this may also be a cause of misfortune."

The man had a fine son who loved horses, and while he was riding the new horse, he fell off and broke his leg.

The villagers felt sorry for the man and his son. "What a disadvantage to have a broken leg. It will leave the boy crippled," was the common sentiment.

"Perhaps even this will one day turn out to be a blessing," said his father.

About a year later, the northern Hu invaded China. All able-bodied young men were required to take up arms and fight against the invaders. There was a terrible war, and as a result, around the border regions, nine out of ten young men died. This man's son was not required to join in the battles because he was crippled, and so both the boy and his father survived.[2]

As this story suggests, it may be wiser to delay our judgments and face what we must face in the present, leaving the future to take care of itself. If we tend to look to the past, let us, as Nephi did, remember how good the Lord has been to us and then we will have sufficient strength for the day and the evil thereof (see Matthew 6:34).

—ɯ—

If men come unto me I will show unto them their
weakness. . . . And my grace is sufficient for all men that
humble themselves before me; for if they humble themselves before me, and have faith in me, then will I make
weak things become strong unto them.

Ether 12:27

How Many Loaves
Have Ye?

Bearing Burdens with Ease

Most of the time when I face adversity, I am hoping the Lord
will remove the cause of my affliction. That is what I pray for, but
there is another equally justifiable prayer and one usually more in
line with what the Lord would do for us. It is the prayer for
strength. This prayer is most often answered by the Lord's increas-
ing our ability to face the adversity before us. Perhaps the ultimate
example of this principle comes from the Book of Mormon, when
the people of Alma the Elder are in bondage to the Lamanites
under the immediate tyranny of Amulon. "So great were their afflictions that they began to cry mightily to God." Amulon forbids
them the consolation of vocal prayer, so the people "did not raise
their voices to the Lord their God, but did pour out their hearts to
him; and he did know the thoughts of their hearts" (Mosiah 24:10,
12).

The Lord's response to these prayers is rather interesting. "Lift up your heads and be of good comfort," he tells them. "I will covenant with my people and deliver them out of bondage" (Mosiah 24:13). If I had been among them, I would have assumed that the deliverance would be quick in coming, almost immediate. They are a righteous people. They have prayed. The Lord has power, so we might think he would move the project forward and end the affliction. But the Lord responds in another manner. "I will also ease the burdens which are put upon your shoulders, that even you cannot feel them upon your backs . . . and this will I do that ye may stand as witnesses for me hereafter, and that ye may know of a surety that I, the Lord God, do visit my people in their afflictions" (Mosiah 24:14).

While this is comforting, I think I would probably respond to these words with something like, "Strengthening is great, Lord, but what I really had in mind was the end of my affliction. I appreciate that You will visit me during my times of trouble, but couldn't we just get it over with? I can bear witness of Your kindness and mercy just as well in ending my affliction as I can in being strengthened."

In the account of Alma's people, the Lord seems to be aiming at a certain attitude we should maintain while facing affliction. It is difficult to cultivate, and it may take a number of adversities to produce this attitude in us and then to finally master it. It may take us a lifetime to acquire this quality, but it returns high dividends. Notice the description of the people's attitude to the Lord's strengthening: "And now it came to pass that the burdens which were laid upon Alma and his brethren were made light; yea, and the Lord did strengthen them that they could bear up their burdens with ease, and they did submit cheerfully and with patience to all the will of the Lord" (Mosiah 24:15).

Developing an approach to life wherein we submit cheerfully—and with patience—is very challenging. When we do, it almost does not matter what the final outcome is. Alma's people were soon released from their burdens. In some lives, however, the burden may not be removed, perhaps, until death. What we hope for is to develop the patience and cheerfulness manifested by Alma's people. Our burdens may not be removed. But when they are not, the Lord can instill in us the strength to carry them with ease, even cheerfully.

Five Loaves for Five Thousand

When we feel we are inadequate for our present adversity, we can find encouragement in the knowledge that the Lord will multiply our sufficiencies. Many times in the scriptures the Lord tells us, in effect, that when we are lacking, when we feel we don't have enough of whatever is needed, he will multiply what we have and make it equal to the demand. Notice that this principle does not teach that the Lord will supply all that is lacking. That may be true in some cases, but more commonly the Lord takes what we already have and makes it more than adequate.

We turn to these scriptural stories with the conviction that what God did for those who lived in the past he will do for us. Twice in the New Testament Jesus fed many people from a small amount of bread. There are similar stories in other books of scripture. We can turn to all these stories of adversity and find in them a pattern of more being demanded than one has. Here is the scriptural blueprint:

1. Someone has an insufficiency. There is not enough of something. In the New Testament examples, it is bread. "Give ye them to eat," Jesus said (Mark 6:37).

2. The individual in need is distressed, confused, unable to find the solution, and appeals for help—from God, the Savior, a prophet. "From whence can a man satisfy these men with bread here in the wilderness?" the disciples ask (Mark 8:4).

3. The person asking for help is always required to contribute what he or she has. This is an important point. In the stories of the feeding of the five thousand and the four thousand, only Mark makes that essential distinction. The other Gospels leave out that very important element, but it is present in Mark.

"He answered and said unto them [his disciples], Give ye them to eat. And they say unto him, Shall we go and buy two hundred pennyworth of bread, and give them to eat? He saith unto them, How many loaves have ye? go and see. And when they knew, they say, Five, and two fishes" (Mark 6:37–38). There was a deliberate search made at the request of the Master—"go and see."

In the account of the feeding of the four thousand, we find the same inquiry being made. "And his disciples answered him, From whence can a man satisfy these men with bread here in the wilderness? And he asked them, How many loaves have ye? And they said, Seven" (Mark 8:4–5).

This third step is the key. The Lord wants us to look for what we have, for what we can contribute to the solution of the problem. We can expect him to ask that question. There is something powerful in an individual searching his or her own life, wisdom, and experience for the needed strength or insight. There is redemption just in the discovery. Often that is all that is needed, but when it is not, the miracle follows.

4. God multiplies what we have and makes it sufficient for the circumstance. Five thousand are fed "as much as they would" until "they were filled" (John 6:11, 12).

5. Because God is gracious and good, he always gives beyond our need. He multiplies what we have and then some. The disciples take up "twelve baskets" after the feeding of the five thousand, and they take up "seven baskets" after the feeding of the four thousand. (Mark 6:43; 8:8).

"Not Any Thing . . . Save a Pot of Oil"

Let us look at another example of this principle. It is found in the Old Testament, in a story from the life of the prophet Elisha. There are types and shadows of Christ's ministry all through the Old Testament, and this is one of them. During his ministry, he repeated several miracles like those of Elisha and other well-loved prophets. The pattern here is a truth needed by all, because we all face adversity and find ourselves lacking.

"Now there cried a certain woman of the wives of the sons of the prophets unto Elisha, saying, Thy servant my husband is dead; and thou knowest that thy servant did fear the Lord: and the creditor is come to take unto him my two sons to be bondmen" (2 Kings 4:1).

This woman has a problem. She does not have enough to pay her debt, and her sons' labor is demanded as satisfaction for the debt. "Elisha said unto her, What shall I do for thee? tell me, what hast thou in the house?"

There is that all-important question—what do you have to contribute? True to human nature, she minimizes what she has, seeing mostly what she lacks. You can almost hear the despair in her voice as she replies to Elisha. "Thine handmaid hath not any thing in the house, save a pot of oil. Then he said, Go, borrow thee vessels abroad of all thy neighbours, even empty vessels; borrow not a few" (2 Kings 4:2-3).

How many times when we face our own struggles do we focus on what we lack and say, "I don't have anything. I have only a pot of oil (or any other small, seemingly useless asset). What good will that do me?"

Yet with timid faith the woman borrows vessels from all the neighbors. She takes them into her room and shuts the door. The next words are simply marvelous when we apply them to our own lives. "And she poured out" (2 Kings 4:5). That is what we all need to do—pour out! As she poured out, the oil was multiplied, and every vessel was filled. The strength we need most often comes as we pour out, when we give what we have to the Lord. Strength is supplied in the pouring process. We will often be amazed at our own resilience and adaptability.

"Then she came and told the man of God. And he said, Go, sell the oil, and pay thy debt, and live thou and thy children of the rest" (2 Kings 4:7). Here we find the part of the pattern that shows the Lord's graciousness. He gives beyond our need. Perhaps the faith we exercise by pouring out increases our capacity. He will fill our insufficiencies and beyond!

These truths are taught on another occasion in the life of Elisha when he feeds a hundred men with twenty loaves of barley (2 Kings 4:42–44). Thus this chapter begins and ends with a multiplication miracle. It is hard to miss!

We also see the same truths taught earlier, in the life of Elijah, when he promised the widow of Zarephath that "the barrel of meal shall not waste, neither shall the cruse of oil fail" (1 Kings 17:14).

We frequently go to the Lord, pleading, "Lord, I don't have enough wisdom for this problem. I don't have it! I need wisdom! Will you give it to me?"

His answer is to ask us what wisdom we do have and asks us to give it to him. He multiplies it, makes it sufficient for our need, and then adds to it, making us wiser than before. Perhaps instead of a lack of wisdom, it's a question of lacking enough strength— emotional strength, spiritual strength, physical strength. Maybe we are dealing with a troubled child, or have a problem in our marriage, or a concern in our employment or schooling. Do we feel we have a calling that is beyond our ability? Is it a matter of insufficient talent or intellectual capacity? Whatever it is, if we will offer to God what we do have, he can multiply it, make it sufficient, and beyond. Let us pour out.

—𝕞—

And though the Lord give unto you the bread of
adversity, and the water of affliction, yet shall not
thy teachers be removed into a corner any more,
but thine eyes shall see thy teachers.

Isaiah 30:20

When Paradise Is Lost

"Of Every Tree"

In the Garden of Eden, the Lord taught our first parents one
of the grand secrets for living a happy and fulfilled life. Everything
depended on where their eyes were focused. "Of every tree of the
garden thou mayest freely eat," the Lord offered (Moses 3:16). This
was followed by the prohibition concerning the fruit of the tree of
the knowledge of good and evil. I used to think the choice in the
Garden of Eden was between two trees—the tree of life and the tree
of the knowledge of good and evil. But the choice was really a
choice between every other tree and the tree of knowledge of good
and evil. In proportion to all the trees they could freely partake of,
including the tree of life, how restrictive was one forbidden one? If
we live our lives focused on the many things we have and can do
rather than on what we are forbidden to have or do, we will be

grateful, contented, and happy. That is one of the very first lessons God teaches in the scriptures.

Satan now enters the garden, but his approach to the trees is vastly different. To Eve he says, "Yea, hath God said—Ye shall not eat of every tree of the garden" (Moses 4:7). Satan wants Eve to center her attention on the one tree she cannot partake of. He suggests that God is limiting her. There is something desirable which God won't allow. The adversary wants us to focus on those things we do not have and cannot do. If we choose his point of view, we will live discontented, bitter, ungrateful, and rebellious lives. Everything depends on the concentration of the mind and heart, on where we choose to focus our attention.

In time Adam and Eve leave the garden. Having lost paradise, they can live their whole lives in the shadow of that loss or they can focus on what they still have, and what they have is considerable. They have each other. Given the choice of Eve or Eden, Adam chose Eve. I think it instructive that immediately after the Lord explained the consequences of their choice to Adam and Eve, Adam turned to his wife and affirmed both her name and her calling. "And Adam called his wife's name Eve, because she was the mother of all living" (Moses 4:26). He focused on what he still had, not on the lost paradise of Eden.

From time to time, each one of us will have to leave a desired or accustomed Eden. We lose the paradise of past comfort levels. Adversity drives us from our garden existence where everything seemed perfect. It is at these moments that we must focus on what is left, not on what we've lost.

We are also invited to see the possibilities in our new situation, even though it may be a lone and dreary world in comparison to our past paradise. We do not know how Adam and Eve felt as they left the Garden of Eden, but the phrase "lone and dreary world" suggests they could not help but compare their former world of beauty and ease to their new one of thorns and thistles. It takes them a while, but in time both Adam and Eve comment on what they have gained through adversity. "My eyes are opened," Adam declares, "and in this life I shall have joy" (Moses 5:10). He says, in effect, Even in a lone and dreary world I can have joy. I have gained knowledge through experience. Eve echoes his realization, concentrating primarily on her children. "We never should have had seed," she says, "and never should have known good and evil, and the joy of our redemption, and the eternal life which God giveth unto all the obedient" (Moses 5:11). Adam spoke of joy in this life; Eve projected forward to the eternities. They are centered on what they have gained. New possibilities have opened up.

"Stronger Than the Powers of Hell"

Learning is one of the best ways to cope with adversity. If Adam and Eve learned about good and evil and the gladness of posterity, Joseph Smith learned something about himself while in Liberty Jail, perhaps the lowest point in his life. What he learned, we can all learn, and the knowledge is extremely valuable.

In his letter from Liberty, Joseph told the Saints what the whole miserable experience had taught him. "You will learn," he wrote, "by the time you have read this, and if you do not learn it, you may learn it, that walls and irons, doors and creaking hinges, and half-scared-to-death guards and jailers, grinning like some damned spirits, lest an innocent man should make his escape to bring to light the damnable deeds of a murderous mob, *are calculated in their very nature to make the soul of an honest man feel stronger than the powers of hell.*"[1]

We learn that we are resilient. We learn that we can live in a world of imperfect, even inhumane, people and events. We learn that we do not have total control over our lives, and yet we do have control over our attitude toward our adversity. We can survive in a world that can break our hearts but not our spirits. We can use our innate strength to adapt, to see what is left, what new possibilities are offered, how we can build happiness on another foundation. We need not complain nor return in kind the evils we endure. We learn that goodness and decency, compassion and kindness will always, in the long run, be stronger than their opposites.

We feel the lessons learned in Liberty from another letter written by the Prophet Joseph Smith just a few brief days before he left for Carthage with his brother Hyrum. His calming faith was born in the crucible of past difficulties, and it maintained him at this last hour. Writing to his uncle, John Smith, on 17 June 1844, Joseph said: "I write these few lines to inform you that we feel determined in this place not to be dismayed if hell boils over all at once. We feel to hope for the best, and determined to prepare for the worst."[2]

The Murmurers

Laman and Lemuel never learned the lesson of turning their backs to the past and hoping for the best in the future. Their murmuring nature arose from their inability to give up the perceived paradise that they left behind in Jerusalem. They centered their thoughts on what they had lost, not on what remained to them or on future possibilities. "These many years we have suffered in the wilderness, which time we might have enjoyed our possessions and the land of our inheritance; yea, and we might have been happy" (1 Nephi 17:21). In this verse is the crux of their murmuring, rebellious nature.

Such thinking looks for someone or something to blame. Laman and Lemuel seem unable to take responsibility for their own emotions or for their response to their wilderness existence. It is always someone else's fault, and thus their anger and dissatisfaction with life increases. "Their anger did increase. . . . Yea, they did murmur against me, saying: Our younger brother thinks to rule over us; and we have had much trial because of him" (2 Nephi 5:2–3). The exact opposite is true.

What is so fascinating about the account of Laman's and Lemuel's conflicts is in the contrast we see between their response to their adversities and that of Nephi. Nephi adapts to his new situation, looks for the possibilities, and sees gratitude everywhere. "And so great were the blessings of the Lord upon us, that while we did live upon raw meat in the wilderness, our women did give plenty of suck for their children, and were strong, yea, even like unto the men" (1 Nephi 17:2). He takes responsibility for his own attitude. There is no one to blame. Life is life—he deals with it. "Why am I angry because of mine enemy? Awake, my soul! . . . Rejoice, O my heart, and give place no more for the enemy of my soul" (2 Nephi 4:27–28).

We see a similar pattern when examining the murmuring of the children of Israel during the Exodus. Even though Egypt meant bondage for them, they preferred its accustomed security to the freedom with faith offered by Moses. They never forgot Egypt, an ironic paradise to hold in the memory if ever there was one. "We remember the fish, which we did eat in Egypt freely; the cucumbers, and the melons, and the leeks, and the onions, and the garlick: But now our soul is dried away: there is nothing at all, beside this manna, before our eyes" (Numbers 11:5–6). What a telling statement on the state of their adversities. Melons were preferable to manna, fish to freedom. They could see "nothing at all," because their eyes were full of Egypt, a paradise of bondage. Are our own adversities crushing us, our souls "dried away" because we cannot see the bread of heaven for the former feasts of Egypt?

It would take a new generation who did not have to forget the taste of garlic and leeks in order to build a people prepared for the promised land. They learned to adapt to the harsher realities of the wilderness, to rely on themselves, to see the possibilities their God was offering them. As they prepared to cross the Jordan River into a new life, Moses emphasized what the Lord had taught them through their wandering in the wilderness: "He humbled thee, and suffered thee to hunger, and fed thee with manna . . . that he might make thee know that man doth not live by bread only, but by every word that proceedeth out of the mouth of the Lord doth man live" (Deuteronomy 8:3). There are things more important than meeting daily physical needs. How often does the loss of trifles like these cause unhappiness? Perhaps the only way God can teach us what is really significant and needful, what is eternal, is to take away the melons and the cucumbers that we might learn to savor the taste of his manna.

Accepting Limitations

We need to be somewhat cautious about the next scriptural clue dealing with adversity. It has to do with accepting limitations and occasionally adjusting downward our expectations of ourselves or others. Satisfaction, fulfillment, and happiness may not totally depend on our initial aspirations or goals. We may be able to live and live joyfully with much less than we originally thought. I say we need to be careful with this because it can become an excuse for apathy, loss of faith, or bitterness. The expression "settling for less" may come to mind, but that is not what we are talking about. A man's reach should exceed his grasp, as Robert Browning wrote,[3] but it must not cloud reality.

We do not know what the aspirations and hopes were of the twenty-four Lamanite daughters before they were kidnapped by Amulon and the wicked priests to be their wives, but the women's later defense of their husbands suggests they had reached some sort of reconciliation both with their lives and with their mates. Leah knew from the beginning of her marriage that she was not Jacob's first choice for a wife, but she found a measure of contentment and joy in her many sons.

Moses gives us perhaps the best example of this scriptural hint to earthly survival. Moses had the highest hopes for his people, and was not alone—God shared those hopes. At Sinai the Lord gave the Israelites what we often call the higher law. They heard the Lord's voice speaking the Ten Commandments from Sinai and agreed to keep this basic moral law. Moses then returned to the summit to receive the higher law. Within a few short weeks the people had forgotten their covenant and built the golden calf. When Moses returned from the mountain, he broke the tablets in a symbolic demonstration that the original covenant was not in force. But neither the Lord nor Moses gave up on the people. Moses' hopes and expectations had to adapt to the realities and limitations of the people he led. Because the Israelites were unable to keep the higher law, the Lord gave them another they had a better chance of keeping, one filled with daily practices and reminders rather than a fuller law that depended on the Holy Spirit to adapt truth and principles to moral decisions.

"And the Lord said unto Moses, Hew thee two other tables of stone, like unto the first, and I will write upon them also, the words of the law, according as they were written at the first on the tables which thou brakest; but it shall not be according to the first, for I will take away the priesthood out of their midst; therefore my holy order, and the ordinances thereof, shall not go before them" (JST Exodus 34:1).

The Lord referred to this moment in the Doctrine and Covenants while explaining the responsibilities and blessings of the Melchizedek Priesthood. "And this greater priesthood administereth the gospel and holdeth the key of the mysteries of the kingdom, even the key of the knowledge of God. Therefore, in the ordinances thereof, the power of godliness is manifest. . . . Now this Moses plainly taught to the children of Israel in the wilderness, and sought diligently to sanctify his people that they might behold the face of God; but they hardened their hearts and could not endure his presence" (D&C 84:19–20, 23–24). The Lord did not wash his hands of the whole affair; rather, "the lesser priesthood continued," one centered on "the preparatory gospel" (D&C 84:26). The word *preparatory* is a positive word. It suggests that more is coming. God had not given up on his people but made an adjustment, a downward adjustment, though one still noble and fulfilling, preparatory to yet greater.

We see a similar example with Samuel, the Israelite prophet, when the people demanded a king. Both Samuel and the Lord knew that was not wise. But the people were determined, so a king was allowed. God chose "Saul, a choice young man, and a goodly" (1 Samuel 9:2), and Samuel assured the people that even with a king, things could still work well if they continued to follow the Lord's commandments, "for the Lord will not forsake his people" (1 Samuel 12:22). "Moreover as for me," Samuel said, "God forbid that I should sin against the Lord in ceasing to pray for you: but I will teach you the good and the right way" (1 Samuel 12:23).

People we love may disappoint us. Life may take from us our most anticipated joys. We may need to face the reality of our own limitations, but none of these need destroy our ability to adjust our dreams and to do so positively. It does not need to be all or nothing. There are many acceptable degrees between these two edges of joy's continuum where we can love and laugh and live while still hoping and striving and preparing for something better.

The Lebanese poet Kahlil Gibran wrote a tiny parable to illustrate this principle. It is concise and to the point with a touch of humor, and the truth it teaches gives scope to life's adversities. It is titled "The Fox":

"A fox looked at his shadow at sunrise and said, 'I will have a camel for lunch today.' And all morning he went about looking for camels. But at noon he saw his shadow again—and he said, 'A mouse will do.'"[4]

In the morning of our lives we may cast long shadows and therefore expect great things of ourselves, but added experience, wisdom, and the passage of time may foreshadow another reality that can give just as much happiness. Let us continue to dream of camels but not be in despair when noon arrives and our shadow has diminished—"A mouse will do."

"O My Son Absalom"

Often the real tragedies of life teach us that what we had considered an adversity was really only a difficulty, a nuisance, an inconvenience, even if the stresses and burdens it laid upon us seemed significant. For years David was chased from forest to mountain to desert and back again throughout the land of Israel by a jealous, power-obsessed Saul. This was surely adversity. During this time he was rebuffed in his request for supplies by Nabal, which threw him into a rage. Perhaps that was the straw that broke the camel's back. He had had enough, and someone was going to pay.

Abigail, Nabal's wife, fell on her knees before David pleading that he not kill her household for the insult her husband had launched at him. "A man is risen to pursue thee," she said, "and to seek thy soul: but the soul of my lord shall be bound in the bundle of life with the Lord thy God. . . . And it shall come to pass, when the Lord shall have done to my lord according to all the good that he hath spoken concerning thee, and shall have appointed thee ruler over Israel; that this shall be no grief unto thee, nor offence of heart unto my lord, either that thou hast shed blood causeless, or that my lord hath avenged himself" (1 Samuel 25:29–31).

David thought his adversity was so great that he was ready to shed the blood of innocent people for an insult given to him by a man who "was churlish and evil in his doings" (1 Samuel 25:3). Abigail knew that the present difficulties were not crippling and that they would come to an end. Jonathan knew this also and often encouraged David. I wonder, reading the story of David's life, how he later viewed those early days of trial after enduring the deep tragedies that befell his children.

When David sinned against Bathsheba and Uriah and faced the subsequent death of his infant son—that was tragedy. The rape of his daughter Tamar by her half-brother Amnon—that was tragedy. The subsequent murder of Amnon by Tamar's brother, Absalom— that was tragedy. It all came to a climax when Absalom rebelled against David, was executed by Joab after their battle, and word reached David of the death of his son. Here is tragedy, distress, and adversity at its most painful conclusion, perhaps one of the most heartrending passages in holy writ: "And the king was much moved, and went up to the chamber over the gate, and wept: and as he went, thus he said, O my son Absalom, my son, my son Absalom! would God I had died for thee, O Absalom, my son, my son!" (2 Samuel 18:33).

I frequently have to ask myself if the adversities that seem so debilitating and disappointing to me are, in comparison, merely troubles, problems, difficulties, and inconveniences but not tragedies. Yet even real tragedies, whether witnessed or endured by ourselves, serve to connect us to humanity, filling us with compassion, pity, forgiveness, gratitude. No thinking, feeling person ever reads the story of David or that of Saul and concludes, "Well, they deserved what they got!" Rather, their adversities and the sorrow that follows their decisions bind them to us, their fellowmen. This is what it sometimes means to be alive, to be human, to fail, to fall. There, but for the grace of God, go I. I can shoulder my own burdens with humility and courage and move into the future. Eden may be lost, but we will taste the fruit of the tree of life hereafter.

CHAPTER TWELVE

—∿—

Behold, I send an Angel before thee,
to keep thee in the way, and to bring thee into
the place which I have prepared.

Exodus 23:20

THE SWORD OR THE ANGEL

Peter and James

Acts 12 records the arrests of two Apostles—Peter and James.
They were the leaders of the early Church. These were men upon
whom Jesus had laid the weight of carrying his gospel forward. The
outcomes of their imprisonment, however, were vastly different.
Therein we have food for thought as we continue to explore what
the scriptures can teach us about adversity.

"Now about that time Herod the king stretched forth his hands
to vex certain of the church. And he killed James the brother of
John with the sword" (Acts 12:1-2). This is a terse beginning, a
blunt factual statement, without detail, reporting the death of
James. Realizing that this act pleased the Jewish authorities, Herod
prepared to execute Peter also. "When he had apprehended him,
he put him in prison, and delivered him to four quaternions of soldiers to keep him" (Acts 12:4). Peter was quite a prize for Herod,

and the enemies of the Church were savoring the anticipated death. But in Peter's case their expectations were disappointed.

Luke, the author of Acts, tells us that "prayer was made without ceasing of the church unto God for him" (Acts 12:5). Do we think that prayer had also been "made without ceasing" for James? It's safe to assume it had, but James received the sword, nonetheless. Perhaps his death inspired a deeper intensity in the Church's petitions in behalf of Peter? Perhaps the execution had come quickly? Whatever the case, the prayers for James were not answered in the same way as they would be for Peter.

Luke gives us a detailed description how Peter was saved from Herod's grasp: "Peter was sleeping between two soldiers, bound with two chains: and the keepers before the door kept the prison. And, behold, the angel of the Lord came upon him, and a light shined in the prison: and he smote Peter on the side, and raised him up, saying, Arise up quickly. And his chains fell off from his hands" (Acts 12:6–7).

Peter is instructed to put on his sandals and wrap his cloak about him and follow the angel. "And he went out, and followed him; and wist not that it was true which was done by the angel; but thought he saw a vision. When they were past the first and the second ward, they came unto the iron gate that leadeth unto the city; which opened to them of his own accord: and they went out, and passed on through one street; and forthwith the angel departed from him" (Acts 12:9–10).

That is a remarkable story, an inspirational account of the mercy of God in delivering one of his servants from the severest form of adversity. When I read the accounts of the martyrdom of James and the saving of Peter, I cannot help but ask, "Why did James get the sword and Peter the angel?" Was Peter more important to the Church than James? I think not. Did the Church pray with greater love and fervency for Peter than for James? I doubt it. Did the Lord love Peter more? Impossible. Was Peter more righteous and therefore more deserving of divine intervention? Of course not. Was it James's time to go and not Peter's? Perhaps.

Whatever the cause or causes, the two intertwined stories have deep relevance. I think they were placed in the same chapter, side by side, to reveal that relevance.

When we face our own adversities—when life "stretch[es] forth [its] hands to vex" us, do we ever want the sword? No! We hope and pray for God to send us the angel. Metaphorically speaking, we want to see the shining light of the approaching heavenly messenger, feel the chains drop from our hands, be led as in a vision past the guards, past the gate, and into the street of freedom—but what if instead we get the sword?

I think of a ward in which two families were afflicted by cancers growing in the bodies of two young mothers. The members of the ward fasted. Priesthood blessings were bestowed. Names were lovingly and faithfully placed on the prayer rolls of the temple. One mother was miraculously saved. The cancer, to the amazement of the attending physicians, diminished and then disappeared. Joy and gratitude pervaded this home, and faith was vindicated. In the other home, sorrow dominated as the mother slowly lingered in pain-wracked life. The cancer grew, overtook healthy organs, and in time she passed away.

One cannot help but ask why. When these things happen, we may be tempted to assume reasons that are not true. Surely both families were loved by the Lord. One was not more important than the other. Each was equally deserving and righteous. Each was in need of a mother's loving care to nurture young children. The prayers of ward members and priesthood blessings were offered with the same intensity of concern, the same expression of faith and petition. But one family got the sword and the other the angel.

Depending on the circumstances, many question the seeming injustices of life. Is there any controlling sense to some of these things? Why are wonderful young couples, deeply desirous of children, unable to conceive? We teach as an essential truth of the gospel that Latter-day Saint families should try to bring the Lord's children into nurturing homes of faith and love. Yet we see many faithful couples denied the joys of parenthood while children are born every day into abusive and destructive home environments. From time to time we all must face—and some of us more constantly—the harsh realities of an un-ideal life.

We may not understand or be able to explain why the sword comes to one and the angel to another, but the stories in Acts 12 can be wonderfully comforting simply because they involve two of the most beloved and righteous of Christ's servants. We cannot but assume James was equally important, equally loved, equally prayed for as was Peter, but the sword came to him and the angel to Peter. From another point of view, James may have been the blessed one, for he returned to his Lord; Taoists, who prefer to withhold judgment, might argue thus. Sometimes in life we get the sword, and sometimes we get the angel. Most often we need to leave it at that. We simply do not know, but we can eliminate from our thinking what is not real, and the examples of James and Peter help us do so.

We can enhance the perplexity of James's situation in particular by looking at an earlier arrest of the same two Apostles. When they were preaching at the temple, the authorities "laid their hands on the apostles, and put them in the common prison. But the angel of the Lord by night opened the prison doors, and brought them forth, and said, Go, stand and speak in the temple to the people all the words of this life" (Acts 5:18-20). This is almost identical to Peter's experience in Acts 12. So, at one time in his life, James did get the angel, but we do not always. There may be an equality of swords and angels for us all. James's situation could not have changed dramatically in the short interval of time between Acts 5 and Acts 12.

Another question presents itself in the account of Peter's escape. What happened to the guards who were assigned to watch him? "When Herod had sought for him, and found him not, he examined the keepers, and commanded that they should be put to death" (Acts 12:19). Did "keepers" mean only the commanders of the prison, or did that term include all four quaternions of soldiers? A quaternion was a detachment of four soldiers, so four quaternions would total sixteen men. The Lord must have considered this eventuality when he sent the angel. If Peter escapes, men will be executed, whether a few or sixteen. Which of us can account for these things sufficiently? Yet our conclusions must not be negative, either concerning ourselves or others we know and love.

Ananias and Sapphira

A story told by Luke in the early chapters of Acts relates to the story of Peter and James in an interesting way. Early converts to the Church were selling their land and donating the proceeds to the Apostles. Luke introduces Barnabas to us with his consecration. There is, however, a couple who want the outward show of consecration without the full sacrifice. Their names are Ananias and Sapphira.

After selling their land, they "kept back part of the price," giving the remainder to Peter. Peter, filled with the Spirit, confronts

Ananias. "Why hath Satan filled thine heart to lie to the Holy Ghost?" Ananias, hearing Peter's words, "fell down, and gave up the ghost: and great fear came on all them that heard these things" (Acts 5:2-3, 5). Ananias was quickly buried without his wife's knowledge. A short time later she went in to meet with Peter. "Tell me," he asked her, "whether ye sold the land for so much? And she said, Yea, for so much. Then Peter said unto her, How is it that ye have agreed together to tempt the Spirit of the Lord? behold, the feet of them which have buried thy husband are at the door, and shall carry thee out. Then fell she down straightway at his feet, and yielded up the ghost" (Acts 5:8-10).

This is an unusual story, particularly in the New Testament, where mercy rather than harsh judgment tends to dominate. What are we to do with an account of this nature? Aside from its eccentric quality, it raises the old questions again. If the Lord is going to take someone for evil choices, why not take Nero, Hitler, Stalin, or some other evil person who brought upon so many so much misery, cruelty, torture, war, and death?

I do not know how to answer that question. Perhaps we are not meant to ask. God has his reasons. We may not be able to comprehend such choices at the hands of Deity. Even if the Lord desired to answer the questions, we might not be able, in our present state, to comprehend the wisdom of the answer. Abraham learned that God could be boldly approached, even questioned. He was a God who could give beyond one's most fervent hopes and dreams, as he did by blessing Abraham and Sarah with the birth of Isaac. And yet he could also demand unbearable, even impossible sacrifices, as he did by asking Abraham to offer Isaac upon Mount Moriah.

Can we accept God on these terms? Can we put our trust in him? Can we commit to him? Can we learn to live with some ambiguity? We are prone to expect, almost demand, concrete, stable, and formulaic answers. Yet even in the gospel there are some uncertainties. But they need not shake our faith. What are the alternatives? Apostasy, rejection, apathy, accusation. Do we turn away?

One thing is certain. True faith brings sweeter fruit, creates nobler lives, and offers more comforts than their opposites. We may need to conclude as did Nephi: "I know that he loveth his children; nevertheless, I do not know the meaning of all things" (1 Nephi 11:17). We may need to say as did Alma, "These mysteries are not yet fully made known unto me; therefore I shall forbear" (Alma 37:11).

Erasmus of Rotterdam, one of the most famous humanist writers of the sixteenth century and a man with a profoundly beautiful understanding of Christianity, wrote a letter to his friend Martin Dorp. Therein he said: "Part of our knowledge lies in accepting that there are some things we cannot know, and a great many more where uncertainty is more beneficial than a firm standpoint."[1]

CHAPTER THIRTEEN

—⟶ꟷ—

God is our refuge and strength, a very present
help in trouble. Therefore will not we fear, though
the earth be removed, and though the mountains
be carried into the midst of the sea.
Psalm 46:1

THAT OUR BURDENS
MAY BE LIGHT

Only the Necessary Things

Paul's missionary success among the Gentiles was beyond anyone's expectations. The Gentiles of Asia Minor, Greece, Syria, and
Rome would become the recipients of many of Paul's letters. But
the integration of Gentile converts into the Church created a problem. Should they be required to live the dietary laws, celebrate the
holy days, and participate in other practices peculiar to the formerly
Jewish Christians? Many of these were amazed to hear the doctrine
that their Messiah had come to save the world, not just members of
the house of Israel who were scattered around the Mediterranean.

A conference was held in Jerusalem under Peter's direction to discuss what would be required of the various nationalities who accepted
the Savior. The conference concluded that Gentile converts need not
comply with the requirements of Jewish law; however, Church authorities, in letters to the Gentile converts, asked them to do certain things.

In one letter, recorded in Acts 15, we find a beautiful verse, a wonderful indication of how the Lord feels about the adversities and burdens of life: "For it seemed good to the Holy Ghost, and to us, to lay upon you no greater burden than these necessary things" (Acts 15:28).

What a lovely message! It is an approach to life that parents, leaders, and anyone with responsibility for someone else can learn from. I believe with all my heart that the Lord has no desire to lay upon us, or to allow life to lay upon us, any greater burden than those that may be necessary for our growth and progression. He desires our happiness. Creating joy is at the very core of his being.

I do not believe that every adversity that comes into our lives does so because it is necessary in his grand plan. I am confident that we face many things that the Father of us all would rather we avoid. The cruelties of men, the ravages of nature, the weaknesses of our physical bodies may bring to us burdens not in the majestic plan of a loving God. Life brings them, life in its imperfect scope, life in a fallen world, yet a life that still contains immeasurable joys and fulfillment. I believe that God does not burden us with many of the adversities that we face—but that does not mean that he cannot or will not turn them to our advantage. God knows that the joy we hunger for—which is in our eternal nature—cannot be fully realized here in mortality. We were made for another place, a greater glory: "Wherefore, fear not . . . for in this world your joy is not full, but in me your joy is full" (D&C 101:36).

Jesus, who understood his Father perfectly, said to us, "Come unto me, all ye that labour and are heavy laden, and I will give you rest. Take my yoke upon you, and learn of me; for I am meek and lowly in heart: and ye shall find rest unto your souls. For my yoke is easy, and my burden is light" (Matthew 11:28–30). God desires that our burdens be light, that our adversities be short-lived, that our trials be easy, that our lives be restful. Life is not always this way, but I cannot ascribe every trial that comes to the will of the Lord. We will face some "necessary things," which he allows, but having faced them, we will find that life is designed to be joyful and full of gladness.

That is why we turn to our Father in Heaven in our adversity. We know instinctively that he wishes our adversity to end as fully as we do. With his wisdom and power, we may trust that he will help us change adversity to a positive outcome. Above all, he will see that we learn from whatever we suffer.

In the Broadway musical *Camelot*, Arthur asks Merlin what to do when one is sad. Merlin's answer is revealing: "Learn!" Learning is the language of the Father. We are here to learn, especially to learn the difference between good and evil. That is what godliness consists of—the ability to always distinguish between good and evil and to ever choose the good.

May the Lord bless us that we may learn—for what we learn is all we can take with us at death—the lessons gained in mortality, lessons that sometimes must be gained through adversity. We must know, deep within ourselves, that God would not have us burdened but would have us face only "these necessary things."

The Old Testament prophet Nahum testified beautifully and concisely: "The Lord is good, a strong hold in the day of trouble; and he knoweth them that trust in him" (Nahum 1:7). The main role of our God is as a helper, a healer, and a refuge, rather than a tester or one seeking proof for advancement. I believe he is not the great examiner of heaven but a tutor instructing his beloved students. We may trust him, for he is good. As we face our several adversities, may Alma's prayer be our prayer, for ourselves and for all others: "And then may God grant unto you that your burdens may be light, through the joy of his Son. And even all this can ye do if ye will. Amen" (Alma 33:23).

—◆—

NOTES

Introduction: The Commonality of Adversity

1. "I Know My Father Lives," *Children's Songbook* (Salt Lake City: The Church of Jesus Christ of Latter-day Saints, 2000), 5.

Chapter One: Thou Knowest the Greatness of God

1. Bible Dictionary, s.v. "Isaac" and "Ishmael."
2. Bible Dictionary, s.v. "Manasseh."
3. Bible Dictionary, s.v. "Ephraim."
4. C. S. Lewis, *The Great Divorce*, in *The Complete C. S. Lewis Signature Classics* (New York: HarperCollins, 2002), 338.
5. Andrew D. Olsen, *The Price We Paid: The Extraordinary Story of the Willie and Martin Handcart Pioneers* (Salt Lake City: Deseret Book, 2006), 156.

Chapter Two: It Is Finished

1. William Shakespeare, *Macbeth*, in *William Shakespeare: The Complete Works, Second Edition*, ed. Stanley Wells and Gary Taylor (Oxford: Clarendon Press, 2005), act 5, scene 5, lines 23–27.

Chapter Four: Thy Friends Do Stand by Thee

1. Joseph Smith, *History of The Church of Jesus Christ of Latter-day Saints*, ed. B. H.

Roberts, 2d ed. rev. (Salt Lake City: The Church of Jesus Christ of Latter-day Saints, 1932–51), 3:293.

2. Smith, *History of the Church*, 3:286.

Chapter Five: Thou Art Not Yet as Job

1. See Elie Wiesel, *The Trial of God (as it was held on February 25, 1649, in Shamgorod): a Play in Three Acts* (New York: Random House, 1979).

Chapter Seven: In the Days When the Judges Ruled

1. William Shakespeare, *Macbeth*, in *William Shakespeare: The Complete Works, Second Edition*, ed. Stanley Wells and Gary Taylor (Oxford: Clarendon Press, 2005), 4.3.225–26.
2. William Shakespeare, *Richard the Third*, in *William Shakespeare*, ed. Wells and Taylor, 4.4.22–24.
3. William Shakespeare, *Romeo and Juliet*, in *William Shakespeare*, ed. Wells and Taylor, 3.5.196–97, 209–10.
4. "A Child's Prayer," copyright © 1984 Janice Kapp Perry, in *Children's Songbook* (Salt Lake City: The Church of Jesus Christ of Latter-day Saints, 2000), 12. Used by permission.
5. Fyodor Dostoevsky, *The Brothers Karamazov*, trans. David McDuff (New York: Penguin, 1993), 321.
6. Dostoevsky, *Brothers Karamazov*, trans. McDuff, 417.
7. William Shakespeare, *King Lear*, in *William Shakespeare*, ed. Wells and Taylor, 5.3.20–21.

Chapter Nine: Sufficient unto the Day

1. Jane Austen, *Pride and Prejudice* (New York: Penguin, 1996), 348.
2. See, for example, Derek Lin, *The Tao of Daily Life* (New York: Penguin, 2007), 56–57.

Chapter Eleven: When Paradise Is Lost

1. Joseph Smith, *History of The Church of Jesus Christ of Latter-day Saints*, ed. B. H. Roberts, 2d ed. rev. (Salt Lake City: The Church of Jesus Christ of Latter-day Saints, 1932–51), 3:297; emphasis added.
2. Smith, *History of the Church*, 6:485–86.
3. See Robert Browning, "Andrea del Sarto," in *Robert Browning: Selected Poems* (New York: Penguin Books, 2004), 117.
4. Kahlil Gibran, *The Collected Works* (New York: Everyman's Library, 2007), 18.

Chapter Twelve: The Sword or the Angel

1. Erasmus, "Letter to Martin Dorp," in *Praise of Folly*, trans. Betty Radice (London: Penguin, 1971), 231.

INDEX

Abigail, 135
Abraham: on sacrifice of Isaac, 55, 74; on
    questioning God, 87; on approaching
    God, 142
Absalom, 3-4, 135-36
Abundance, 76
Accusation, 63
Accuser, 55
Achan, 42
Action, 41, 43, 44, 112
Adam and Eve, 4, 127
Adversity: many types of, 1, 3-5, 117, 134;
    turned to blessings, 9, 50, 76, 136;
    dealing with, 45, 49, 94, 103, 128-29;
    problems of, 87, 107-8, 137
Affliction: as blessing, 16, 18, 107; causes of,
    17, 73; help from Lord in, 76, 106, 120
Agency, 87
Allegory of olive tree, 75-76
Alma the Elder, 119-21
Alma the Younger, 73, 75, 143, 146
Alyosha, 93-94
Ammon, 106
Amnon, 135

Amulon, 119-21, 132
Ananias, 141
Angel(s), 38, 79, 138-41
Atonement, 5, 80, 94
Austen, Jane, 113

Backpacking, story of, 67
Benjamin, story of, 89, 115
Bennett, Elizabeth, 113
Betrayal, of Jesus, 28-29
Blessing(s): from adversity, 4-5, 12, 18;
    affliction as, 16; all adversity turned to,
    50, 107; of others, 78, 97, 116; counting
    our, 112; prophets and, 115, 130;
    sometimes have to wait for, 117-18
Bodil, story of, 19-21
Book of Remembrance, kept by God, 68
Brain cancer, 1-2
Brothers Karamazov, The, 93-94
Browning, Robert, 132
Bull, Mrs. Norman, letter to, from Joseph
    Smith, 49
Burdens: of Jesus, 29, 84; lightened, 46,
    120, 145; types of, we are not meant to
    carry, 103-4

INDEX

Camelot, 146
Cancer: brain, 1-2; 139-40
"A Child's Prayer," 88
Christ, love of, 8, 78-79
Compassion, 36, 81
Concubine and Levite, 88-90
Consecrate, meaning of, 16
Cordelia, 95
Courage, 50

Darcy, Mr., 113
Daughters of Ishmael, 104-5
David, 3, 46, 83, 134-36
Despair, 92
Discouraged, 37, 40-41
Dishonesty, of Ananias and Sapphira, 141
Dog, story of, dying, 2
Dorp, Martin, 143
Dostoevsky, Fyodor, 93

Elijah: on pleading for death, 4; story of,
    37-40; Lord's instructions to, 45, 52,
    112; and widow of Zarephath, 123-25
Elisha, 123-24
Endure, 23, 27, 70
Enoch, 24, 81-83
Ephraim, meaning of, 14
Erasmus of Rotterdam, 143
Esau, 3, 113-14
Eternity, 83
Exodus, 75, 130
Experience, 9, 17, 73

Faith, 18, 22, 93-94, 143
Forgiveness, 14, 30, 116-17, 136
Fox, story of, and mouse, 134
Friends, 48-52, 57, 59, 69, 72, 85
Future, 104, 106-7, 118

Gibran, Kahlil, 134
Glacier National Park, 67
Glory, 8, 10-11
God: and reasons for adversity, 7, 16,
    61-62, 82, 142; how, helps us, 33, 42,
    76-77, 122, 124; and Job, 54-58;
    characteristics of, 64, 70, 72
Good, 8-9, 13-15, 19, 129
Guilt, 15, 39, 63, 81, 117

Habakkuk, 65-67, 70
Handcart companies, 19-21
Handcart reenactment, 21
Hannah, 46, 100, 109
Happiness, 34, 82
Healing, 92, 112
Hell, 94
Help, 107-8, 122
Holy Ghost, 74, 132, 145
Hope, 3, 9, 48, 102, 110, 112, 121, 134
Humility, 9-12, 131

"I Know My Father Lives," 5
Injustice, 65
Instructions, 40-41, 43
Insufficiency, 121, 124
Interpretation of dreams, 32
Isaac, 13, 55, 142
Isaiah: on the Lord helping us, 24, 27, 46,
    83; on the Savior as a man of sorrows,
    73
Ishmael, 13, 104-5
Ivan, 93-94

Jacob, son of Isaac, 3, 15, 113-16
Jacob, son of Lehi, 15, 75-76
James, story of execution, 137-41
Jeremiah, 4, 69, 71
Jericho, 42
Jerusalem, 77, 105, 144
Jesus: trials of, 4, 27-29, 51-52, 57; feels
    our sorrow, 77-78; story of feeding
    thousands, 121-23
Job: story of, 4, 53-61, 60, 70; trust in
    God, 56, 65
John, on our day, 24-25, 27, 79-81, 97
Jonathan, 46-47, 135
Joseph, in Egypt, 4, 13-15, 15, 32
Joseph, son of Lehi, 15
Joshua, story of, 42-43, 52
Joy, 27, 49, 128, 134, 145
Judas, 28-20, 52
Judgments, 71, 118
Juniper tree, 38-39
Justice, 62, 65

Kidnapping of daughters of Shiloh, 90
Kindness, 91

INDEX

King Lear, 95
Knowledge, 128

Lamanites, Christ's visit to, 78-79
Lame child, 35-36
Lazarus, 4, 77-78, 80
Leah, 3, 113, 132
Learn, 128, 146, 129, 146
Lehi, 15, 34, 104-5, 111
Letter(s), 49-50, 129
Levite and concubine, 88-90
Lewis, C. S., 18-19
Liberty Jail, 23-24, 47-50, 85, 87
Life, 61, 65-67, 140
Limitations, 131
Love, 13, 46, 50, 59, 92-94, 101
Luke, 109, 138

Macbeth, 35, 86
Macduff, 86-87
Malachi, 67, 70
Man in China, 117-18
Man, lame from birth, 97
Man, at pool of Bethesda, 4
Manasseh, 14
Manna, 41, 131
Martin and Willie handcart companies,
   19-21
Mary and Martha (of Bethel), 4, 77, 80-81,
   98
Mary Magdalene, 79-81
Mary (mother of Jesus Christ), 30, 75
Memories, 113
Mercy, 73, 83
Mitya, 93-94
Mormon, 101
Moroni, 55, 101, 111
Mortality, limitations of, 5
Mortensen, Bodil, story of, 19-21
Moses, 24, 37, 40-42, 45, 52, 76-77, 108
Mourn with those that, 74
Murmuring, 41, 104, 129-30
Mysteries, 143

Nature, 17
Nebuchadnezzar, 83
Nephi, 4, 71, 110-11, 143
Nephites, Christ's visit to, 78-79

Nirvana, meaning of, 36

Offering, 124
Opposition, 7, 34

Pain, 3, 5, 11-12, 62, 73
Parable, Hindu, 33-36
Partridge, Bishop, 48
Past, 105, 113
Patience, 8-9, 13, 15, 106, 120
Paul: things suffered by, 7-13; on learning
   from experiences, 15, 31-32, 62, 66; on
   being strengthened by the Lord, 74, 85,
   109
Peace, 24, 29
Peter, 28, 51, 79-81, 97, 144, 137-41
Pharaoh, 14, 26, 115
Pioneer girl, story of, 19-21
Possibilities, 127-28
Prayer(s): of pleading, 47, 70-71, 78, 96,
   119; answers to, 88, 108-9; of prophets,
   110, 134, 138
Pregnant woman, story of, 98-99
Price, paid by others, 22
Pride and Prejudice, 113
Prison, escape from, 138
Problems, solving, 43, 70, 122
Promises, Jacob reminds God of, 114
Prophets: on being discouraged, 37, 40,
   47-50, 60; told to take action, 40-41,
   43, 110, 112

Question(s), 39, 61, 64-65, 67-68

Rachel, 3, 113, 115-16
Reconciliation of Jacob and Esau, 115
Residue, 81
Ruth, 91-94

Sacrifice, 21, 95, 142
Sagebrush, story of gathering, 20
Samuel, 133
Sapphira, 141
Sarah, 55
Satan, 17, 54-58, 63, 81, 127, 142
Scriptures, 3-4, 6, 88, 91, 106
Selfishness, 90

INDEX

Shadrach, Meshach, and Abed-nego, 83-84

Shakespeare, 35, 86, 94

Sin, 54

Smith, Don Carlos, letter from, 48

Smith, Emma, letter from, 48

Smith, Hyrum, 129

Smith, Joseph: on needing comfort, 65, 70; in Liberty Jail, 4, 23-24, 27, 47-50, 85, 108; in Sacred Grove, 107-8; visit by Moroni, 111; on feeling stronger than the powers of hell, 128

Sorrow, known by God, 12, 76, 78, 84, 101, 104, 111, 139

Stories: of author's wife's brain cancer, 1-2; of author's dog dying, 2; of types of adversity in scriptures, 3-5; of Paul, 7-13; of Joseph in Egypt, 13-15; of Bodil Mortensen, 19-21; of gathering sagebrush, 20; of handcart reenactment, 21; of Joseph Smith in Liberty Jail, 23-24, 47-50; of betrayal of Jesus, 28-29; of wishing tree, 33-36; of lame child, 35-36; of Elijah and priests of Baal, 37-38; of Elijah under juniper tree, 38; of Moses, 40-42; of Joshua, 42; of Hannah, 46; of Job, 53-61; of Sarah, Abraham, and Isaac, 55; of Habakkuk, 65-67; of backpacking in Glacier National Park, 67; of author's friends, 69; of *The Trial of God*, 70; of Lazarus, 77-78; of Christ's visit to the Nephites and Lamanites, 78-79; of Mary Magdalene, 79-81; of Enoch, 81; of Shadrach, Meshach, and Abed-nego, 83-84; of Levite and concubine, 88-90; of Ruth, 91-94; of *The Brothers Karamazov*, 93-94; of King Lear and Cordelia, 95; of Mary anointing Jesus, 98; of young pregnant woman, 98-99; of death of Ishmael, 104-5; of Joseph Smith in Sacred Grove, 107-8; of Jacob, son of Isaac, 113-14; of Benjamin, 89, 115; of man in China, 117-18; of Alma the Elder, 119-21; of Jesus feeding thousands, 121-23; of Elisha, and widow, 123-24, and feeding one hundred men, 124; of Elijah and widow

of Zarephath, 124-25; of the Exodus, 130; of fox and mouse, 134; of David and Absalom, 134-36; of Peter and James, 137-41; of cancer, 139-40; of Ananias and Sapphira, 141

Strength, 10, 108, 119, 123

Submit, cheerfully, 120

Success, promised in future, 106

Suffering: purpose of, 21, 50, 53-54, 62; end of, 26, 36; Job's, is without cause, 56; problem of, 70, 82, 90; agency as cause of, 87

Sword, 137-41

Tears, 24-25, 27

Temptation, 73

Tempted, meaning of, 74

Ten Commandments, 26, 132

Testimony, 21

The Brothers Karamazov, 93-94

The Trial of God, play by Elie Wiesel, 70

Thrive, in midst of trials, 75

Tomb, Mary Magdalene at, 79-81

Tragedies, types of, 135-36

Trial(s): part of the refining, 2, 10, 96; will have an end, 23, 52, 84; story of, of God, 70; thrive in midst of, 75

Trust, of Job in God, 56, 63-64, 66, 69

Truths, taught by contrasts, 91

Tutor, 5, 10

Understanding, 143

Unhappiness, 81

Wait, 66

Weeping, 81-83

Wicked, prospering of, 65, 67-68, 90

Widow; story of Elisha and oil, 123-24; of Zarephath, 124-25

Wiesel, Elie, story of trial of God, 70

Willie and Martin handcart companies, 19-21

Wishing tree, story of, 33-36

Woman with issue of blood, 4

Young, Brigham, 20